Spirit & Flame

Spirit & Flame

AN ANTHOLOGY OF CONTEMPORARY
AFRICAN AMERICAN POETRY

Edited by

Keith Gilyard

SYRACUSE UNIVERSITY PRESS

Copyright © 1997 by Syracuse University Press
Syracuse, New York 13244-5160

All Rights Reserved

First Edition 1997
97 98 99 00 01 02   6 5 4 3 2 1

*This publication was made possible by a grant
from the Office of Academic Affairs, Syracuse University.*

Library of Congress Cataloging-in-Publication Data
Spirit & flame : an anthology of Contemporary African American poetry / edited by
Keith Gilyard. — 1st ed.
p.   cm.
ISBN 0-8156-2730-0 (cloth : alk. paper). — ISBN 0-8156-2731-9
(pbk. : alk. paper)
1. American poetry—Afro-American authors.   2. Afro-Americans—
Poetry.   3. Gilyard, Keith, 1952–
PS591.N4S65   1997
811'.54080896073—dc20   96-35253

Manufactured in the United States of America

To the memory of
Shayk Suliaman El-Hadi
(1936–1995)

He was called midflight, but flight it was.

Contents

Daniel Gray-Kontar

Duriel Harris

Safiya Henderson-Holmes

gale jackson

Major L. Jackson

Harriet Jacobs

Valerie Jean

A. Van Jordan

Karen Williams

Niama Leslie JoAnn Williams

Demetrice A. Worley

Al Young

Kevin Young

Acknowledgments

This collection owes much to the vision of Robert Mandel, director of Syracuse University Press, who was most eager to see it happen. My thanks to him and his entire staff. I would also like to acknowledge the generous and collective spirit of the poets contained herein. Much of the material came in through the grapevine, as I had hoped it would. The most frequent question asked of me was whether I had contacted some other poet who was deemed by the questioner to be deserving.

My deepest gratitude goes to Juanita Horan, who diligently prepared most of the manuscript, and to the staff of The Syracuse University Writing Program, who graciously cut me the necessary slack on that job to get this one done.

In addition, I gladly thank the following for permission to reprint material: "Theory On Extinction or what happened to the dinosaurs?" from NOMMO. Copyright © 1991 by Kenneth Carroll. Reprinted by permission of the author. "History as Trash" and "Traditional Post-Modern Neo-HooDoo Afra-Centric Sister in a Purple Head Rag Mourning Death and Cooking" from *Good Sense & the Faithless* by Michélle T. Clinton. Copyright ©1994 by Michélle T. Clinton. Reprinted by permission of the author and West End Press. "Black Boys Play the Classics," "Family Secrets," "1994 Inventory," and "From a Letter: About Snow" from *Prairie Schooner*. Copyright ©1994 by Toi Derricotte. Reprinted by permission of the author. "Vacation" from the *New Yorker*. Copyright © 1994 by Rita Dove. Reprinted by permission of the author. "In the Old Neighborhood" from *Selected Poems*, by Rita Dove. Copyright © 1993 by Rita Dove. Reprinted by permission of the author. "The Drama" from the recording *Scatterrap/Home*, by The Last Poets. Copyright © 1994 by Suliaman El-Hadi. Reprinted by permisson of Jemeelah El-Hadi. "This Poem," "Waitin on Summer," "Green Boots n Lil Honeys," and "You So Woman" from *We Are the Young Magicians*, by Ruth Forman. Copyright © 1993 by Ruth Forman. Reprinted by permission of Beacon Press. "and sometimes i hear a song in my hand" from *Catalyst*. Copyright © 1991 by Harriet Jacobs. Reprinted by permission of the author. "imagination in flight: an improvisational duet" from *Catalyst*. Copyright © 1994 by Harriet Jacobs. Reprinted by permission of the author. "Children of the Future" from the recording *On the One*. Copyright © 1996 by Jalaluddin Mansur Nuriddin. Reprinted by permission of the author. "The Art of the Nickname" from *Hootenanny*. Copyright © 1995 by Dominique Parker. Reprinted by permission of the author. "I am not the walrus" and "El Paso Monologue" printed with the permission of Ishmael Reed. "The Spice of Life," "Height, Breadth, Depth," "Sunrise on the River," "New Orleans Rainbow," "Spiritual Geography," and "Makes You Go Oohhh!" from *Essence* magazine. Copyright © 1995 by Kalamu ya Salaam. Reprinted by permission of the author. "Poem for July 4, 1994" and "This Is Not a Small Voice" from *Wounded in the House of a Friend,* by Sonia Sanchez. Copyright © 1995 by Sonia Sanchez. Reprinted by permission of Beacon Press. "Good Nights" from *Typing in the Dark,* by Saundra Sharp. Copyright © 1991 Saundra Sharp. Reprinted by permission of the author. "Mississippi Blues" from *Palanquin/TDM* and *The Real News*. Copyright © 1993 and 1994 by lamont b. steptoe. Reprinted by permission of the author. "Window Shopping" from the *Journal of New Jersey Poets*. Copyright © 1996 by lamont b. steptoe. Reprinted by permission of the author. "Laurel Street, 1950," "Blues at 1," and "Sister Lakin and Lally" from *Fly with the Puffin,* by Dorothy Perry Thompson. Copyright © 1995 by Dorothy Perry Thompson. Reprinted by permission of the author. "Domestic Work, 1937" from the *Gettysburgh Review*. Copyright © 1996 by Natasha Trethewey. Reprinted by permission of the author. "Secular" from *Callaloo*. Copyright © 1996 by Natasha Trethewey. Reprinted by permission of the author. "Naola Beauty Academy, New Orleans, Louisiana 1943" and "Drapery Factory, Gulfport, Mississippi 1956" from *Agni*. Copyright © 1993 by Natasha Trethewey. Reprinted by permission of the author. "Collection Day" from the *Massachusetts Review*. Copyright © 1996 by Natasha Trethewey. Reprinted by permission of the author. "& Syllables Grow Wings There," "One for Charlie Mingus," and "Avalanche" from *Avalanche,* by Quincy Troupe. Copyright © 1996 by Quincy Troupe. Reprinted by permission of the author. "For Paula Cooper" from *Writing Our Way Out of the Dark,* edited by Elizabeth Claman. Copyright © 1995 by Jackie Warren-Moore. Reprinted by permission of the author. "Sub Shop Girl," "Providence Journal V: Israel of Puerto Rico," "Brooklyn," and "Easy Living" from *Timber and Prayer: The Indian Pond Poems,* by Michael S. Weaver. Copyright © 1995 by Michael S. Weaver. Reprinted by permission of the author. "Blue Monday," "Ravel: Bolero," "Written in Bracing, Gray L.A. Rainlight," "Fifty-Fifty," and "The One Snapshot I Couldn't Take In France" from *Straight No Chaser,* by Al Young. Copyright © 1992, 1993, and 1994 by Al Young. Reprinted by permission of the author. "Reward," "Southern University, 1962," and "Eddie Priest's

Spirit & Flame/Birth & Name

We talked about poetry conventions and festivals. We talked about big anthologies. We talked about something like *Black Fire*. Whenever we poets gathered to chart our course in the lean years, that is, the period (1975 or so until now?) when corporate publishers pulled the plug on the Electric Black Poetic, we knew we had serious literary work to do beyond merely writing poems. Wishing to maintain an aesthetic fervor to help propel progressive political struggle, some of us founded journals and magazines; others began small presses and/or published our own manuscripts. Despite such vital movement, of which I was a part, I still harbored the desire, because anthologies are a key vehicle of dissemination, to edit a compendium that would hold up to a big, bad, promising, encompassing, Black, revolutionary, lyrically strutting ideal. I haven't totally fulfilled that urge yet, but *Spirit & Flame: An Anthology of Contemporary African American Poetry* takes much of the edge off. It is my attempt, limited though it is by certain logistics, to indicate the considerable range of contemporary African American poetry, a project not attempted in over twenty years. In 1987, Cheryl Wall asked a group of prominent African Americanists at a conference in Philadelphia, "What constitutes Afro-American poetry today?" None knew,and I suspect her question would provoke the same response a decade later. To simply document or popularize current African American poetic tendencies, then, would be reason enough to do a book of this sort. Scholars, teachers, students, and laypersons all could benefit. But I also think of all the poets who have yearned, much as I have yearned, to connect, to know, and to act.

Spirit & Flame is keenly aware of its most famous predecessors. By the late 1960s, a mix of anthologies like *The Book of American Negro Poetry,* edited by James Weldon Johnson (1922), *American Negro Poetry,* edited by Arna Bontemps (1963), and *Black Voices* (only partly verse), edited by Abraham Chapman (1968), comprised a canon of twentieth-century African American poetry. All three remain in print, and among them one can find the more notable poems by the likes of Paul Laurence Dunbar, William Stanley Braithwaite, Claude McKay, Frank Horne, Georgia Douglas

Johnson, Langston Hughes, Countee Cullen, Gwendolyn Bennett, Sterling Brown, Melvin B. Tolson, Fenton Johnson, Waring Cuney, Owen Dodson, Naomi Long Madgett, Mari Evans, Margaret Walker, Gwendolyn Brooks, and Robert Hayden, as well as Johnson and Bontemps.

The editorial mission Johnson set for himself was to prove that African Americans were capable of high art, for it was his belief that "no people that has produced great literature and art has ever been looked upon by the world as distinctly inferior." Today this view seems a bit tenderminded and not wholly appropriate in the context of hardcore American racism. In any event, no anthologist since has felt the need to make the case for a Black poetry anthology on quite the same grounds. Bontemps, for example, was simply concerned with capturing the essence of a voluminous and varied outpouring of African American poetry. Chapman claimed he was up to much the same in *Black Voices,* but the collection was not particularly adventuresome in terms of poetry, not for 1968. Of the twenty-four poets featured in *Black Voices,* only Lance Jeffers and Lerone Bennett, Jr. had not appeared in either Johnson's or Bontemps's anthologies. Approximately half of the poems appeared in the earlier works. Nonetheless, *Black Voices* served to round out the canonical picture up to 1968. If some establishment figure broached the subject of Black poetry, one could be pretty sure of the creative direction in which he or she was pointing. Not to say that none of the above poets were radical; some were. They were all, however, familiar—which is why *Black Fire: An Anthology of Afro-American Writing* was the big poetry news that year.

A large multigenre collection, *Black Fire,* edited by LeRoi Jones (Amiri Baraka) and Larry Neal, contained some two hundred sixty pages of poetry devoted, in line with an evolving Black aesthetic, to celebrating Blackfolk and villifying their enemies. In addition to Jones and Neal, poets such as Charles Anderson, Calvin Hernton, Lethonia Gee, K. William Kgositsile, A. B. Spellman, Sonia Sanchez, Ron Welburn, Welton Smith, Rolland Snellings (Askia M. Touré), Kirk Hall, Jay Wright, Yusef Iman, Victor Hernandez Cruz, Kuwasi Balagon, and Bobb Hamilton stretched, jettisoned, or exploded so-called mainstream poetic conventions. Neal confirmed as much in the afterword:

> most of the book can be read as if it were a critical reexamination of Western political, social and artistic values. It can be read also as a rejection of anything that we feel is detrimental to our people. And it is almost axiomatic that most of what the West considers important endangers the more humane world we feel ours should be.

Black Fire set the tone for anthologies that followed on its heels. None ignored its passionate politics and instrumental view of art. Dudley Randall's still-popular 1971 entry, *The Black Poets,* featured *Black Fire* contributors, Baraka, Spellman, Sanchez, Neal, Smith, and Iman, alongside another emerging group, which included Johari Amini, June Jordan, Carolyn Rodgers, Ishmael Reed, Don L. Lee (Haki Madhubuti), and Nikki Giovanni. Randall, in his mid-fifties at the time, really appreciated the agenda set by the younger poets. He published thirty poems by Baraka and Sanchez alone. Chapman's sequel, *New Black Voices* (1972) highlighted Baraka, Cruz, Hall, Jeffers, Neal, Welburn, and Wright as well as important comtemporaries such as Jayne Cortez, Eugene Redmond, Michael Harper, Quincy Troupe, Al Young, and Val Ferdinand (Kalamu ya Salaam). In 1974, the revised edition of *American Negro Poetry* was published, expanded to include Calvin Hernton, Larry Neal, Audre Lord, Nikki Giovanni, and several others. However, in a decidedly conservative move, it was decided not to account for the nominal and poetic conversion of Baraka. The poems in the original edition, which were taken from *Preface to a Twenty Volume Suicide Note* (1961), were not replaced.

Other anthologies that were published between 1968 and 1974 include Clarence Major's *The New Black Poetry* (1969), Ted Wilentz and Tom Weatherly's *Natural Process* (1970), June Jordan's *soulscript* (1970), Orde Coombs's *We Speak As Liberators* (1970), Woodie King's *Black-Spirits* (1972), and Arnold Adoff's *The Poetry of Black America* (1973). These compilations, those mentioned in the paragraph above, and a significant strand of performance poetry by artists such as The Last Poets and Gil Scott-Heron pretty much formed the Black poetry canon of the sixties.

Although Black poets continued to proliferate, they stopped being published in large, well-distributed books. The overall Black vibe was considered too strong. The more fiery volumes were soon out of print. We received slim play in the mainstream anthologies, fared slightly better in the multicultural projects that came into vogue. However, it was not until the 1990s that major anthologies of African American poetry reappeared, a phenomenon that may be linked to the burgeoning Malcolm X (can't beat it, sell it) industry, which would prove to be both an apt and an ironic development, given the influence of Malcolm on poets two or three decades earlier.

The recent books are outstanding in their own right, but none was conceived to be both wide-ranging and contemporary. Instead, their editors generally favored niche strategies. For example, Kevin Powell and Ras Baraka's *In the Tradition* (1992), while pushing the youthful genius of poets like Tony Medina, virtually excludes poets over thirty-five. Charlotte Watson Sherman's *Sisterfire* (1994) incorporates exciting work by Jackie Warren-Moore, Toi Derricotte, Michélle Clinton, Saundra Sharp, gale jackson, Ruth Forman, and others, but is restricted to a female lineup. Michael Harper and Anthony Walton's *Every Shut Eye Ain't Asleep* (1994), although aiming to represent the "entire spectrum of African-American poetic practice," mainly retraces the careers of selected poets since Robert Hayden. Prominent among them is the nation's poet laureate, Rita Dove. E. Ethelbert Miller's wonderful *In Search of Color Everywhere* (1994) is a thematic treatment with a broad historical sweep, although it indeed includes many fine contemporary poets such as Harriet Jacobs, Nikky Finney, Michael Weaver, Lenard Moore, Brian Gilmore, Safiya Henderson-Holmes, and lamont b. steptoe.

As indicated, my goal is to outline (no one book can exhaustively detail it) the African American poetic conversation in the 1990s. Although I have included many of the poets mentioned earlier, there is comparatively little in the way of reprints. My invitation to both established and emerging poets was to feature what they are up to now. And this anthology exists to complement the others that have been and are being produced during what some are calling a latter day renaissance. I was guided in large measure by the question Bontemps raises toward the end of his introduction to *American Negro Poetry,* when he wonders "what spirit will move" the next African American poet. *Spirit & Flame,* as Bontemps might have predicted, reveals that the scene is vibrant and diverse and that there are all kinds of spirits moving African American poets at present. They cherish the Black oral tradition and honor written craft. They riff poetically, spoetically, jazzoetically, if you will, and also pen sonnets. They revere the haiku and love hip hop. They rhyme; they don't rhyme. They reflect what Harper may term "unidentifiably ethnic moments," but the overall tip is strongly political (the flame). They cover issues from the Middle Passage to the Million Man March. And they do it in New York, Philadelphia, Washington, D.C., Cleveland, Los Angeles, New Orleans—as well as in Inkster, Michigan and Rock Hill, South Carolina.

"It's on," as we say in the 'hood, both in the modern sense that some activity is occurring and in the older sense that what is transpiring is also stellar. *Spirit & Flame* derives from all that positive energy, is named by it, and hopes to live its own life well.

Syracuse, New York   *Keith Gilyard*
August 1996

Spirit & Flame

Amiri Baraka

*Amiri Baraka, born in 1934 and raised in Newark, New Jersey, has pro-
duced dozens of literary works including fifteen volumes of poetry. Among
the poetry books are* Preface to a Twenty Volume Suicide Note, The Dead
Lecturer, Black Magic, Hard Facts, Wise, Why's, Y'z, *and* Transbluesency:
Selected Poems 1961–1995. *He has received the Langston Hughes Award
from the City College of New York and is a professor of Africana Studies
at State University of New York at Stony Brook.*

JA   ZZ   :   (The   "Say   What?")
    IS   IS   JA   LIVES

Yes Bees !
God Electric
Come Coming
Fire Jism
S H A N G O
CANTO JONDO
Eternity Power
Living Happiness
S P I R I T L I F E
   WORD SHIP
   The Soul ' s Soul
   SUN THOUGHT BREATH
      Heart Beat
      Is   Going
      Act Play
   Ecstasy's   Now
  Connecting   Endlessness
    REAL TRUE
    LOVE   ALWAYS
  SOUND   ARE
D I G G E R   D I G G I N G
    THE
   WHO BE
    THE
   WHAT WATT
   Seer   Seeing
SO   U   NeeDn't

1

THE KEY
of
M O N K

M U N T U   K U N T U

The Laughing South
NIGHT'S MOTHER
The Crying North
DEY FATHER

"Two Is One"

bottom to Top
Hot   to   Cold
new   to   Old
See   Navy
Sea   Crosser
Trance   Former
Passing going

The
I   Am

The Am Eye

R
B'
Z Z

The Silence of Sound

The   Power
of   Universal
Orgasm

The   Sun's
Nut
The Thunder   The Lightning

The Two Hands
The   Dialectic

WHO
WHERE

The You & I
of Here & There

  THE DOWN UP

  THE BLUE MAN

   WHO

  THE WOMB MAN

  THE HUE MAN

   WHO

   Both
   Yall
    we
   I&I

    The
  US   IS

  I am   Sings

  The Sun God
  Coming out
      His
      Mother

  The Ejaculator
  is The Ejaculation!

  Come Music!

  Visible Thought Herding

   In Walked Dionysius

                                        The Pyramid
                                        change to
                                   The Triangular Trade

                                        The Spell
                                        The Word

                                        Good News
                                        Hip Gnosis

                                   Ghost Murder

                                             Eat Mo
                                        The Grain Crusher
                                                  The Be er
                                                          The Alle
                                        The   Me
                                        See

                                   The   See   Me
                                        The   Me Sea
                                                  Waves

          NIGHT   BLUE
                DAZE
          THE   DERE   DAT

                    The   Eye
                          On

                         The
                              DEATH DEAD!

                         The Living Knowing

                              THE
                              STAY GO

                         CHURCH SPEECH

                         The   STING
                         Of
                              NIGGER PRINTS

MOON'S SON

YOU
I

The So
&
The So

The Where

the
were so

the
Sower

Gravity
The Meaning

the
GO
How

The blue
blown
The Blues
what we blew

Hawk Honk
Black Bird Aflame

The smile rising
the changes the circle
the hole

The Whole

The Hard Empty

The upside down
the twist to
frown

The cold circle checker
The hot opposite the cross the water, before whatnot

the dooji
the vonhz

other stuff
flying anyway

the chord you came in on

The To Where
        The Every
                The body of joy

            The Why

            The Or

            Elegba's Cymbal

        The Y he show you
        Yes, The Cross Roads

                G's Us
            The stiff joint
                The hot poem
                Volcano balls
                The planets humming

            The head circle
            The lost ankh
            The Resurrection
    What John Said
            R e v e l a t i o n s

        We are alive
        We are humans
            r u l ed by h e a t h e n s

    Trying to Remember the formula
                    for killing ghosts

        The underground
            dark blue speed
                star checking

black freedom lady
        the kiss of light

                the orchestra sky
                comet language

        africamemorywhisper

                blowing
                the blown the known
                                what we knew
                                what we blew
                                blues loves us
                        our spirit is ultraviolet

                what we knew
                drumwhich

                the long measure
                my man
                                treeship
                                her son

Becoming the One

Duke's World

Duke's World
        is the explanation
        beauty makes
        the look of understanding
        a new day being so ancient
        brings

        There is an ascendance in Duke. A passage
through which you are pulled, where everything
that lives forever regards itself & lets you know
you can be there always when you are beautiful

There is no ugliness that describes Duke's world
        except what is not

& how it connects to
what is

It is not just the elegance, the irony, the
    sensuous self illumination
    there is a deep happiness
    in Duke's world

What you think is a castle, expansive gardens
is a teacher impeccably in love with
exhaltation & joy. Duke's world
is where we go if we are good.

Kenneth Carroll

Kenneth Carroll, born in 1959 and a native of Washington, D. C., is a founding member of The Spoken Word poetry-performance ensemble and the 8Rock Writers Collective. Currently site coordinator for the WritersCorps and president of the African American Writers Guild, his poetry has appeared in Catalyst, African Commentary, NOMMO, *and* Konch Magazine. *His first book,* So What! *appeared in 1996.*

The Domino Theory
(or Snoop Dogg rules the world)

it is so clear
now
it was right in front of our
ears for all this time & only
now do we see
gangsta rap
gangsta rap did
gangsta rap did it

snoop dogg started the
transatlantic slave trade
doc dre was captain of a
slave ship & eazy motherfuckin
e lead the south to secede

it is all so clear
let the pundits come forth
let the congressional hearings begin
we have found the enemy &
they are dressed in chinos & plaid shirts
& county blues

gangsta rap did it
mc ren was responsible for jim crow
it was ice cube not gov. wallace that
tried to deny us equal rights
it was some forty oz drinking
jehri curl wearing
indo smoking

low riding conspirators that
were responsible for watergate

gangsta rappers,
screaming bitch, ho, skeeze,
defeated the equal rights amendments
it is all so clear
will someone call c delores tucker
tell her we have found the enemy recording
on death row records backed by a funky ass
george clinton groove

it wasn't capitalism, racism, sexism, homophobia
hell naw
it was ice-t & ice cube & just ice
& all them refrigerated gangsta niggas
that screwed up america
nwa imported all the cocaine
to america,
elect ollie north!
it was spice 1 & the South Central Cartel
that traded guns for drugs
before he died
eazy e bashed in nancy kerrigan's knee
killed nicole simpson & ronald goldman
& caused the peso to plummet

let the pundits come forth
call jesse jackson
gangsta rappers are threatening affirmative action
call dick gregory
gangsta rap causes obesity & malnutrition
call ralph nader
gangsta rappers invented the corvair, the chevette, & the pinto
it wasn't the greed of corporate america
it was niggas from compton or long beach or south bronx
it is so clear now
tell the nation of islam
gangsta rappers are the devil not white folk
call the pope gangsta
rappers are the anti-christ
leading us all along the funky road to hell
let the pundits come forth

gangsta rappers killed martin, malcolm, & both kennedys
they started the riots & are responsible for your high
electric bill

we were once blind,
but it is so clear now
ain't it good to know
now we can rest peacefully
as soon as we rid ourselves
of them o.g.s
ain't it good to know
let the pundits come forth,
the cameras are rolling.

Theory on Extinction
or what happened to the dinosaurs?
For my son, Thomas

they were crushed by a gigantic meteor
they froze to death
they starved to death
they didn't wash their hands
they didn't brush their teeth
they got really bad report cards
they believed in gods that did not look like them
they evolved
they assimilated
they died waiting for john brown/jesus christ/& 40 acres & a mule
they died fighting someone else's war
they didn't eat their vegetables
they used porcelana & faded to death
they overdosed on activator
they wanted to be white or arab or greek
they wanted to be anything but dinosaurs
they never read dinosaur history
they never read dinosaur literature
they read ebony and thought they had it made
they read jet and thought they had made it
they joined the republican party
they kept shooting at their own reflections
they got nose jobs/lip jobs/hip jobs
they would do anything for a job

they were scared of revolution
they thought malcolm x was a fashion statement
they never shouted in church
they were mis-educated
they pissed off the great dinosaur gods
they wanted to be like the people who despised them
they were, when they were here, a strange species

they are long gone son,
but you can see them,
at the smithsonian
just ask for the
great
negrosaurus wrecks.

upper marlboro

i know these trees
& how loudly they speak
in a late summer's breeze
accompanied by twittering
birds & the neighing of strong
horses in distant pastures

i know these furtive
creeks & rivers that
wind past green stalks
of corn sweetened by
maryland sunrises on
blue skies

i know this dirt
that cradled my people's feet,
that sucked their sweat & tears,
that demanded blood & life

i know this place
where my uncles ran, raising hell,
refusing to be niggas in a cracka county,
where being a man could leave you hanging
like tobacco in a smoke filled store house

i know this place
where black men kept their shanks sharp,
& their double barrels loaded

i know this place
i have been waiting for it to die
i have been waiting to reclaim it.

something easy for Ultra Black nationalists

so you wanna kill white people . . .
love your family
love your people
love your culture
love Africa
love to learn
love yourself.

it jes' *kills*
them when you
do that.

Short Poem

my hand moved furiously,
trying to capture & convert
scattered thoughts into poetry,
miles blew *bags grooves*
outside the summer sky exploded
in thunderous applause & warm rain

she caressed my hand, sending my words
spiraling toward incomprehension
her tongue trailed a wet, searing path
from my fingers to the lobe of my ear,
all alive now with miles' muted trumpet
sonny rollins' big tenor & her husky whispers

she raised her dress . . . slowly
unfolded herself deliberately
like a patient poet

she meandered on a metaphor,
sauntered on a simile,
exposed brown thighs as perfect
as a langston hughes stanza

my mind evaporated,
my page became weird hieroglyphics
as miles joined percy heath,
they played *but not for me*
she glided, smooth as percy's bassline
toward the darkened bedroom
I couldn't help but think to myself,
as her fragrance lingered to haunt me
that this was gon' be
                    a short poem.

Michélle Clinton

Michélle Clinton, born in 1954, coedited the award-winning Invocation L. A.: Urban Multicultural Poetry. *Her work has been published in numerous journals and anthologies. Her book-length works are* High/Blood Pressure *and* Good Sense & the Faithless.

History as Trash

White yuppies in santa monica go through their attics
    for stuff they will sell on side streets
25¢ for a photo of a colored gentleman in a high collar
    all bourgie & stiff & proper
    like he could read
a portrait rescued from the trash
    by my negro hands I hand picked
a picture of this brother
    shoulda been on his grandbaby's altar
    coulda been my uncle or
    my mother's teacher's preacher
somebody out there in the great
    gap-filled negroid space
in the fascinating stomach hurting trek of africans
    tearing up & building up
all the black energy wound up
right here on my ass
that same afro sticky history
all over the face of this man

photograph prove it

It's because he's a ghost
I think of death
& god & the god of dead negroes
& yo dead negroes bring to mind
spirits & the soul part smaller

than a breath & death again
the way all negroid bodies died:

I believe he died angry
a hurt common to the colored at the time
I believe he died mad
& his madness survives in the air of my world

He coulda been my people
good as the great grand grand momma I don't know
the lost ancestors screaming in my dreams
    & they don't got the good sense of an angel
    & they don't got the patience of a slave
    & they don't share no comforts, no secrets

In honor of the last ancestor
I hang my fists on nails
& sacrifice fried meat
because dead voodoo'n relatives
pick at the violence in my mouth
it's a sin & a shine they dizzy whispers
that crazed hiss lets me know
    death ain't silence
like the jesus clone promises
& the white god of santa monica
or the yuppie deities of indifference
need plenty closet space
& picks out what's useless
& trades it to strangers
for quarters, single bills
whatever they could get.

Traditional Post-Modern Neo-HooDoo Afra-Centric Sister in a Purple Head Rag Mourning Death and Cooking

1.
Traditional:
    that mean has a voice & a person
    you can relate to
    & probably a plot w/ a beginning, middle & end
    & if you don't understand it, the poem don't work
Post-Modern:
    is because of 1945 when the americans dropped
    the first nuclear bomb
    on nagasaki asia

    & got everybody thinking about death of the species
    more problems, more paranoia
Neo-HooDoo:
    1972, *Conjure,* by Ishmael Reed
    deals out of a black bohemian mentality
    also post-nationalist BoHo Nats of new york city
Neo-HooDoo:
    sound a lot like voodoo
    also new, which is not real
Afra-Centric:
    afra-centric
    like first colored was the compliment
    then negro was the compliment
    & nigguh was always the insult
    then change happened
    & black was everything beautiful
    & africa was new
    then nigguh was the precious secret
    then afro-mantic
    now everything
    now afra-centric
    now of course news of the first mother of the first womb
    in the first cave of afra-centric
    africa
Afra-Centric:
    coined by Asungi, womanist artist
Sister:
    this means of a woman
    of the uterus root
In A Purple Head Rag:
Purple:
    a color
    a color like colored like
    nigguh was so black he was blue
    girl was so blue she was purple
    the color purple
    which is Alice Walker which is our time
A Head Rag:
    this is a head rag
    as relaxed
    as home
    as natural
Mourning Death:

Morning:
    as the sound of the first day
Mourning:
    as the sound of hurting for the loss of a dead person
Death:
    as barrier to the spirits
And Cooking:
    as sexual energy
    as communal response
    as human feeling

2.
Morning was the softest hum
an anti-music buzz that ached
in my face when he died
a white boy suicide
in love w/ the evil in elvis
& conjured a heart attack
w/ cigarettes & despair

All the hard & good people
who loved him at a funeral
party freak out

I was about to call
I was ready to wail
    ready to grieve & receive
the basic wisdom to deal w/ the situation
I was trying to be connected
to the black at the bottom of my genes
bad enough to box w/ grief
that plus some impulse to take
care of business & feed people
to taste & stir & season
& pass out plates solid w/ material radiance

It's me thinking
cooking is sometimes a contradiction
folks w/ european privilege
people w/ penis privilege
get happy on the service
& greedy w/ my love
I won't be nobody's mammy

but at a wake when folks mourning
when common & good sense both take a whipping
when understanding sits down, trembles & falls into fits
it's a sin not to cook
it's a sin to hold back any kinda magic you got going

It's me thinking
I gotta come across
so I put an honest drain on my mystery
I cooked
I tried to look good
I ate & danced w/ strangers
I listened for the echo that the dead heart leaves
& wore the color purple

It's me remembering
trying to sing
that plus holding myself
I had to soothe & quiet somebody
& ended up witness
to this pain washing through
a body of people
who came together
because he left us
because he had to
do what all bodies have to do
sometime

which is pass on
let go
& finally say good bye.

William W. Cook

William W. Cook is chair of the English Department and Israel Evans Professor of Oratory and Belles Lettres at Dartmouth College. Author of several critical and creative books, his poetry includes the volume Hudson Hornet and Other Poems *and the manuscript* Spiritual.

Seth Bingham
For Mae

Her going through changes
Takes my mind off
My own hang-ups
And she's aware
She knows she stopped
Being a young stacked filly
Many years ago
She knows
I know
And you know
The conjugation
But we have
Our own reasons
Not to blow her game

Let her try to get a break
Trying to do
Whatever she's trying
To do
When that thing
Her thing
Lays no kind of weight on you.

Let her have a little soup
Since they already
Beat her out of the meat
And we can just
Mind our own business
Because if you're hung up
About anything
If in some shifting way

20

Her thing
Could anyway be yours
Treat that weakness
Like we treat rhythm and blues
Go along with it
Or forget it
That black folk way

Having shucked my way
Past nastiness
You wouldn't recognize
To count
I know how to let her have
A little look the other way

Let her be whomever
And wherever
She might want to be
And call her sister
Every time she tramps your way

The stuff I've looked away from
Every day
Surprises even me.

Still-Life with Woodstove

We did our living in the kitchen.
The woodstove that on holidays burned coal
Stayed in the kitchen though I planned to
Haul it out.
It still sits there.
Broad and black
A burden of cakes and soups
It holds its corner down.

Before the ovendoor
Emilio
With that stillness
Peasant people never shatter
Is teaching me the silence
Of rat traps

Which do not stoop to cheese.
This lesson is both love and manhood
Quietly
After my mother and my sisters
Have fled upstairs aloud
To wait for rats
Who always come to silence.

The gas stove came
And never looked at home.
Too white and thirties art deco
To my artistic eye,
It never found a fitting setting
For its noisy newness.
And we, upwardly mobile
With GE and TV screens,
We did the dining room
French blue and gold.
To brighten shadows in the front,
We moved into our
Resurrected living room
And I forgot almost
The rats who were my rearing.

My mother stands elbow-deep
And brown
Next to the double tubs
That were auxiliary to tables
When oilcloth covers matched.
She did not trust her living
To gas stoves or the living room;
They were too new and up to date
For coffee curtains or for sofabeds.
She never fainted
In distrust of floors,
But shouted in church
Saw visions and to my delight
Spoke Pentecostal tongues to all of us.
What law can liberate the powerful
Or turn the doubter in a new direction?

We moved into the resurrected
Living room

Yet on my canvas I record
The early heat and noise,
The late night silences—
Kitchen, woodstove and
A boy learning to wait
The hunter time of rats.

Spiritual
"How did you feel when you come out the wilderness?"

Like good unprocessed
Negro hair
Touched but not ruined
By the straightening comb
With a healthy dose of Dixie Peach
In this new rain of soul
I want to go home!

I want some wilderness today
I want to get it
So that people will shake
Their heads
And wonder what I put
In that last drink
Or maybe
They'll just smile
At one another
And over my head
With that Lord-have-mercy
Look the sisters get
When it's too bad to touch
And too damned good
To ever let go
That's the wilderness I want

I want to get wilderness
Till people truly wonder
Why they spent
So much time and money
Why they scrimped and saved
To keep me in decent clothes
And everlastingly surrounded

By people who had
Some get up and go
Those up-you-mighty-race folk
Those child-remember-you-were-raised
Mammas
And when I leave the room
I want to hear tongues clucking
As I get hat and go.

And then
Getting the wild and wooley
Wilderness I sent for
I plan to become one
A carrier of the word
A typhoid missionary mary
Who will infect whole city blocks
I want to loosen joints and tongues
Get brothers and sisters to testify
That girdles bras and jockstraps
Are binding and sealed up too tight
Then I want to issue a call
To every soul I saved
Before the end I see
And let them answer me
How did you feel when you
Found out what wilderness could do?

Toi Derricotte

Toi Derricotte, born in 1941, teaches at the University of Pittsburgh. She has authored three collections of poetry, Natural Birth, The Empress of the Death House, *and* Captivity. *In 1993 she received the Distinguished Pioneering of the Arts Award, United Black Artists.*

Black Boys Play the Classics

The most popular "act" in
Penn Station
is the three black kids in ratty
sneakers & tee shirts playing
two violins and a cello—Brahms.
White men in business suits
have already dug into their pockets
as they pass and toss in
a dollar or two without stopping.
Brown men in work-soiled khakis
stand with their mouths open,
arms crossed on their bellies
as if they themselves have always
wanted to attempt those bars.
One white boy, three, sits
cross-legged in front of his
idols—in ecstasy—
their slick dark faces,
their thin wiry arms,
who must begin to look
like angels!
Why do these strings
tremble so sweetly
to our ears?
A: *Beneath the surface we are one.*
B: *Amazing! I did not think that they could speak*
    this tongue.

Family Secrets

They told my cousin Rowena not to marry
Calvin—she was too young, just eighteen,
& he was too dark, too too dark, as if he
had been washed in what we wanted
to wipe off our hands. Besides he didn't come
from a good family. He said he was going
to be a lawyer, but we didn't quite believe.
The night they eloped to the Gotham Hotel,
the whole house whispered—as if we were ashamed
to tell it to ourselves. My aunt and uncle
rushed down to the Gotham to plead—
we couldn't imagine his hands on her!
Families are conceived in many ways.
That night when my cousin Calvin lay
down on her, that idol with its gold skin
broke, & many of the gods we loved
in secret were freed.

1994 Inventory

In a Charleston, South Carolina gift store,
the hottest selling item to this day
is the slave quarters—a little cabin
with a mammy and several pickaninnies.
"We can't keep it in stock!" the saleslady tells me.

From a Letter: About Snow

I am at a retreat house, Still Point, not too far from Yaddo,
and the nun who runs the house told me to look at my face in the
    mirror.
I did, but the only thing I keep seeing is the face of Snow, the huge
    Pyrannese sheep dog.
He's so frightened, they can't let him off his leash!
His human eyes, long-suffering, like a saint who's forgotten how to smile.
I hear the breed is naturally shy, and this one was abused by his previous
    owner.
No wonder he backs away!
But to see a creature so large—120 pounds—so timid!

Once, they say, scared by a deer, he broke his leash and ran.
A mile away a woman stopped with her pick-up truck and he jumped
     right in!
Who knows why the frightened make decisions.
Today I jogged with him, his thick rangy self leading the way.
Now we're sitting in the shade by the community house while I write this
     letter.

Rita Dove

Rita Dove, born in 1952 and raised in Akron, Ohio, was named Poet Laureate of the United States in 1993, the first African American and youngest person ever chosen for the post. Her volumes of poetry include Thomas and Beulah, *a winner of the 1987 Pulitzer Prize*, The Yellow House on the Corner, Museum, Grace Notes, *and* Mother Love. *She is currently Commonwealth Professor of English at the University of Virginia.*

Vacation

I love the hour before takeoff,
that stretch of no time, no home
but the gray vinyl seats linked like
unfolding paper dolls. Soon we shall
be summoned to the gate, soon enough
there'll be the clumsy procedure of row numbers
and perforated stubs—but for now
I can look at these ragtag nuclear families
with their cooing and bickering
or the heeled bachelorette trying
to ignore a baby's wail and the baby's
exhausted mother waiting to be called up early
while the athlete, one monstrous hand
asleep on his duffel bag, listens,
perched like a seal trained for the plunge.
Even the lone executive
who has wandered this far into summer
with his lasered itinerary, briefcase
knocking his knees—even he
has worked for the pleasure of bearing
no more than a scrap of himself
into this hall. He'll dine out, she'll sleep late,
they'll let the sun burn them happy all morning
—a little hope, a little whimsy
before the loudspeaker blurts
and we leap up to become
Flight 828, now boarding at Gate 17.

In the Old Neighborhood

To pull yourself up by your own roots;
to eat the last meal in your own neighborhood.
—Adrienne Rich, "Shooting Script"

Raccoons have invaded the crawl space
of my sister's bridal apartment.
The landlord insists they're squirrels;
squirrels he'll fight, not raccoons—
too ferocious and faggy, licking
their black-gloved paws.

My mother works up a sudsbath
of worries: what if
the corsages are too small,
if the candles
accidentally ignite
the reverend's sleeve?

Father prefers a more
reticent glory. He consoles
his roses—dusts them
with fungicide, spades in
fortified earth. Each summer
he brandishes color
over the neighborhood,
year after year producing
lovelier mutants: these
bruised petticoats, for instance,
or this sudden teacup
blazing empty, its rim
a drunken red smear.

I am indoors, pretending
to read today's paper
as I had been taught
twenty years before:
headlines first,
lead story (continued on A-14)
followed by editorials and
local coverage. Even then

I never finished, snared
between datelines—*Santiago,*
Paris, Dakar—names as
unreal as the future
even now.

My brother rummages upstairs;
I skip to the daily horoscope.
I've read every book in this house,
I know which shelf to go to
to taste crumbling saltines
(don't eat with your nose in a book!)
and the gritty slick of sardines,
silted bones of no consequence
disintegrating on the tongue. . . .

That was *Romeo and Juliet,*
strangely enough, and just as odd
stuffed green olives
for a premature attempt at *The Iliad.*
Candy buttons went with Brenda Starr,
Bazooka bubble gum with the Justice
League of America. Fig Newtons
and *King Lear,* bitter lemon as well
for Othello, that desolate
conspicuous soul.

But Macbeth demanded dry bread,
crumbs brushed from a lap
as I staggered off the cushions
contrite, having read far past
my mother's calling.

The rummaging's stopped. Well,
he's found it, whatever it was.
Bee vomit, he said once,
that's all honey is, so that
I could not put my tongue to its
jellied flame without tasting
regurgitated blossoms.
In revenge, I would explicate
the strawberry:
how each select seed
chose to breed in darkness,
the stomach's cauldron

brewing a host of vines
trained to climb and snap
a windpipe shut—then
watched my brother's eyes as
Mom sliced the red hearts into sugar
and left them to build their own
improbable juice.

I fold the crossword away,
walk back to the kitchen where
she's stacked platters high
with chicken and silvery cabbage.
Lean at the sink, listen to her chatter
while the pressure cooker ticks
whole again whole again now.

Out where the maple tree
used to stand
there once was a tent
(official Eagle Scout issue):
inside a young girl
weeping and her brother
twitching with bravado
because their father, troop leader
in the pitched dark,
insisted they'd love it by morning.

(Let me go back to the white rock
on the black lawn, the number
stenciled in negative light.
Let me return to the shadow
of a house moored in moon light,
gables pitched bright above
the extinguished grass,

and stalk the hushed perimeter,
roses closed around their scent,
azaleas dissembling behind the garage
and the bugeyed pansies
leaning over, inquisitive,
in their picketed beds.

What are these, I'll ask stooping
to lift the pale leaves, and these?

Weeds, my father mutters
from his pillow. *All weeds.*)

Chink. Chink. Sound made by
a starling the first hot morning
in June, when Dad switched on
the attic fan and nothing
stirred—faraway then
a *chink-chip-shiver,*
whittled breath of a bird
caught in the blades.

We each dropped our books
and ran to identify
the first tragedy of the season:
baby sister run down
or a pebbly toad
the lawn mower had shuffled
into liver canapes—
each of us thinking
At least I'm not the one.
Who could guess it would be
a bird with no song,
no plumage worth stopping for?
Who could think up a solution
this anonymous, a switch
flipped on reverse
to blow the feathers out?

"—tea roses, I'd say, plus
a few carnations—and baby's breath,
of course. Are ferns
too much?" I am back
again, matron of honor,
firstborn daughter nodding *yes*
as I wrap bones and eggshells
into old newspaper for burning,
folding the corners in
properly,
as I had been taught to do.

(*Charlottesville, Virginia, June 1993*)

Suliaman El-Hadi

Suliaman El-Hadi (1936–95) was, for almost twenty-five years, a key member of The Last Poets, the internationally renowned poetry ensemble. A native of Philadelphia and a long-time resident of New York City, his poetry is featured on the recordings Chastisement, At Last, Delights of the Garden, Oh My People, Freedom Express, *and* Scatterap/Home. *Selected poems were printed in a volume entitled* Vibes from the Scribes.

The Drama

It's like a terrible dream designed to make you scream
But you know that this is our reality
It's the story of our loss and the devastating cost
To our future and our efforts to be free

Are you ready to relax and gather up the facts
From the things I'm about to say
It's a little tale of drama overlayed with pain and trauma
And curtain call is each and every day

It's about a generation being erased from our nation
Being programmed to self-destruct
And amid the mass confusion they've created the illusion
That the only thing that counts is the buck

It's a tale about our offspring being taught to do the wrong thing
While sucking out a rhythm on a stem
And there are even some brothers who would violate their mothers
And eliminate each other on a whim

It's about the women crying as they watch the children dying
And the playground is the place to buy some dope
The crack vials laying around form a carpet on the ground
Beneath a tire hanging from a rope

It's a script about the old ones being frightened of their own sons
As they watch the family structure disappear
And instead of the protection for the years of their affection
The only thing they got to show is fear

It's a tale about our males being locked away in jails
And the father figure missing from the home
And that old conspiracy to destroy the family
Leaves the women and the children all alone

It's like a terrible dream designed to make you scream
But you know that this is our reality
It's the story of our loss and the devastating cost
To our future and our efforts to be free

It's a tale of unemployment with the limited enjoyment
Of the basic things society should provide
Of the people on the street who so seldom get to eat
And are nonchalantly shuttled to the side

It's the truth about our youth hearing lies instead of truth
And the same distorted image of their worth
And things that should be free in this rich society
Have always been denied them since their birth

It's about their attitudes with the emphasis on rude
And inconsideration is the rule
And youngsters think they're chilling while in fact they're really illing
While ignoring good advice to stay in school

They are victims of oppression and the overall obsession
To always keep people in their place
And those making the decisions seem to parcel out divisions
With the underlying factor being race

Yes it's still the same old story of deception, greed and glory
That brought the ruling classes wealth and fame
And though they tell you things are better—still they leave you wondering
    whether
It is just another title to the game

It's about the morning breeze blowing sneakers in the trees
And garbage is the flowers that you see
It's enough to make you sick when they put you in a trick
Then they tell you the achiever you should be

It's about the people's sadness and their deeply rooted madness
And the indignities to which they must submit

For they know deep down inside this is surely genocide
Just some slavery that possesses fringe benefits

Yes I could go on my friend but this story has no end
It's an everlasting tale of tears and woe
We'll just have to make things right or we'll always be uptight
Because the system is designed for us to blow

It's like a terrible dream designed to make you scream
But you know that this is our reality
It's the story of our loss and the devastating cost
To our future and our efforts to be free

The Tired Man

He stepped into the night aware
Dreams unfurled flashing across the sky.
Outstretched hands felt and grasped the air.
He stared into the night with eyes accustomed to the dark
Accustomed to the sight of violence
Accustomed to the stench of the social mark.
He kicked a beer can, and the still was shattered
Reminding him of the shackles that bound him since birth.
He shed a tear as though it really mattered.
                    And it did.

Kelly Norman Ellis

Kelly Norman Ellis, born in 1964, is a doctoral candidate in English at the University of Kentucky, where she also teaches African American Literature. Ellis is a native of Jackson, Mississippi, and a founding member of the Affrilachian Poets, a writing ensemble of Black writers with strong roots in the Black South. Her work appears in Sisterfire: Black Womanist Fiction and Poetry.

Girl

you wore blue peddle pushers and polka dot tops
saturday mornings
when sun still spoke
through a screenless window above the sink
and the radio rested on its ledge
holding the jive of a dj papa
"the sounds of soul w-o-k-j"
girl
nestled between some newly womanish hips
your hands submerged in lemon joy and breakfast dishes
while the bottoms of bare feet
slid
slopped and
ponied
to four tops
impressions and
dramatics
you were a girl with dixie peach bangs
hugging pink sponge rollers
and cashmere bouquet sprinkled
in the crease of not long opened breasts
who dreamed of boys
talking in poems
and moving in beauty like marvin gaye
will you remember this girl when you are woman
will you remember to love her when she dances
across your dreams and kisses you
like a daughter
on the lips?

Tougaloo Blues

(on a visit to my grandparents' graves
at Tougaloo College Cemetery, May 1994)

For many years I did not make migration
To this mound and ash
This intersection of my flesh
But at thirty my womb is tender
So I have made this pilgrimage
To sacred ground

This is where I meet
Woman boy
Girl man
An ancient embryo
Where waters meet is me

In these wombs of tombstone
I ebb and flow
A cross current
That speaks my names
In plantation moss
And Choctaw refrain

Tougaloo
Tougaloo
Tougaloo
Come home girl

The we and I
Congregate in this quilted ground
Of magnolia fig and muscadine
These be my people singing ancestor blues
And Choctaw croons

Tougaloo
Tougaloo
Tougaloo
Come home girl

My names intersect
Under plantation bone and tear

Where waters meet
I am before I am born
And shall be when I am gone

Tougaloo
Tougaloo
Tougaloo
Come on home girl.

Phantom Pains
For W. L. Slaughter

transplanted southern girls
become fortune tellers in chicago crowds
searching strange men's palms
for mississippi life lines
sleuths
seeking clues
hoping recognition sets in
fondling fingers
sneaking prints
in memphis new orleans
little rock or louisville
bounty hunters pronouncing
"wanted very much alive
mississippi mud crusted callused hands
the color of dark sorghum or
red eye gravy maybe even
lemon pie"
the collective memory of country girls
craves a farmer's touch
so they daydream on
buses
trains and subways
about hands
pulling shrimper's nets in biloxi
peeling sugar cane in pascagola
playing slide guitar
with broken coke bottles in clarksdale
yeah, robert johnson bb king delta blues moaning
hands
trembling on the deacon's bench in vicksburg

boiling salt peanuts in tupelo
casting lines
for buffalo or bream in some hinds county stream
hands
pressing prison bars at parchman or
caressing the pages of dubois at tougaloo
medgar evers richard wright
i'm here to point the way
if you just look up and see
hands
on cold mornings in roxbury
gloved hands
ignite imaginations
spark fantasies
of corn shucking sunflower county hands
of cotton picking choctaw county hands
of ball clutching jackson state and alcorn
sweet swac walter payton
hands
yes, hands with strong as rope veins
growing through the skin
are enough to make
a mississippi woman like me
stop in the middle of a detroit street
convinced i have glanced
pa-pa's knuckles
uncle tj's thumb
brother's pinky
mysterious hands shoved deep in pockets
conjure up phantom pains
grief
for a grandfather's dead
lone licorice
hook clad
ghost hand.

The Boys of Summer

For Chaney, Goodman, and Schwerner
who were murdered the year I was born

through a thicket of piney woods
in a mound of moon crescent dam

you were buried
never meant to rest
only meant to lie
wide eyed
swaddled in ten tons
of communal ground
but earth cradled you
bleeding in her belly
how she must have wailed
when you were forced inside
but she held on
moaning in a field holler
you were never alone
with the bones of other souls
wandering the wombs of mississippi
souls of other lost boys
in watery tombs rolled over
leading a trail to you
that fraternity of emmett till's
you
the boys of freedom summer

and tears
and rock
and choctaw soaked clay
cocooned you
so when earth was broken
to bear again
this time breech birth
faces down
arms outstretched
bearing the marks of crucifixion
the dirges of your bones could be heard
on that perspiring mississippi day
while blue blowflies pirouetted
into your open graves
you told the tale
a black man and two jews
of what the world refused to see
that this was the real beginning of freedom
the opening of a mass grave
called mississippi
the exhuming of corpses

the excavation of lies
the exposing of that mississippi justice

a public autopsy on national tv

yes your bodies were raised from neshoba graves
and your voices were lifted
singing
those who believe in freedom
cannot rest
cannot rest
cause mississippi is still burning
on your funeral pyre
and you still refuse to rest
until all the bodies packed deep
have been swaddled
in a cooling mississippi
freedom
soil.

Robert Farr

Robert Farr, born in 1958, graduated from Syracuse University's New-house School of Communications in 1979 and has been in the corporate world since. Currently a resident of Arlington, Virginia, his work has appeared in several anthologies.

at general Electric, where they eat their/young

what creeps in
to grace the weekend
like a buzzard
slowly circling
over highways,
as i flip down
my mirror shades,
and dismount?
who wears
the cowboy hat
and leather,
as i sign in and walk
like spencer tracy
through the wrought iron
gates?

this is me:
a dramatic Negro
stalking the grounds
of a corporation.
i am on
to fortune five
like an angel
on the back
of a bike.

but how long
can i prolong
the metaphor?
how long
can i be
one of them,

42

before they grill me
with their subtle
questions
and belief turns
with a fury
into doubt?

when
do they realize
i have come here
to destroy them?
to pour sand
into the dark engines
of their economy.
because once again
i become
Prometheus.
and gaze
into their ceremonies,
and steal their fire,
and try
to turn them
out.

then,
they whip me
with the rusty chains
of justice.
and pour a furnace
full of sunlight
into my face.
my back pulls taut
across the sermon
of their rocks;
my shirt
falls roughly
to one side.

once again
the scavenger
blazes with desire.
and tumbles
from the void

>   into the
>   sky:

van/Dyke

under the Protestant gaze of society
i am growing a beard.
some days, it is Martin
singing love songs down in Selma.
some days,
it is a Chippewa,
stumbling through the desert
on the Long March.
some days,
it is Young, Lewis, and Jackson.
but it is using words
to kill.

this is my "i'm tired of all the bullshit"
beard.
this is my
TAKE OFF THE WIG beard.
this is my Baraka beard.
my Harlem nights
in New York City beard,
or standin' on the corner
howlin' at the moon
black
beard.
black beard?
yes.
this is my black beard.
this is my black beard.

this is my "after eight long years
i don't wanna be a Republican"
beard.
this is my
thousand points of light beard.
this is my Methuselah beard,
my pro-Choice beard,
my free love beard,

my condom/pill/and diaphragm beard,
my public beard, my
pubic beard.

this is my beard
for women who love women's
beards.
for men who love men's
beards.
my happy Sunday morning
covered with oatmeal and pancakes beard.
my working in the garden
and not going to no Church beard.
this is my free the slaves
from Sunday School beard.
my tearing down the Temples beard.
my crucifying the Christians beard.
my reliving the Holocaust beard.

this beard is a Buddha beard.
a Yahweh beard.
a Jesus beard.
an Allah beard.
this beard is Vishnu and Shiva
tearing it down
then building it back up again!

this is my/own beard.
this is my
own beard.

but this is also
my pissed-off Indians at Wounded Knee
beard.
my Mandela, Sissulu, and
Biko beard.
my down with apartheid beard. my
continuing sactions against South
Africa beard. my
stand-up-and-fight beard.
my going on strike beard.
my "until the color of a man's skin
makes no more difference

than the color of his eyes"
beard. my beard that says
"until that day, the African continent
will not know peace."
my until *that* day,
it's so-much-
for-wite/people beard.

my scaring off
the white girls beard. my
radical Negro
with big, hairy balls
beard. my
marching through Johannesburg beard.
my marching through the South beard.
my cleaning up the ghetto beard.
my alcoholic Negro beard. my
pregnant little
girl beard. my
standing in the soup line beard.
my sleeping in a shelter
beard.

this beard intends to eat up
your Thanksgiving.
this beard will spoil your July.
because this beard
is rejoining *Black* with *Power*.
this beard is stealing
your sons and daughters.
this beard is Panthers in suburbia.
this beard is riots in the streets.

this beard is:
armed like a dagger,
with saw
teeth.
as it stabs the bluebloods
to the blacktop,
and brings your deacons
to their
knees:

Nikky Finney

Nikky Finney, born in 1957, is assistant professor of creative writing at the University of Kentucky. A native of Conway, South Carolina, her publications include the poetry volumes On Wings Made of Gauze *and* Rice. *She performs and lectures widely and has been involved in the Bluegrass Black Arts Consortium, the Affrilachian Poets, and the National Black Women's Health Project.*

Lobengula: Having a son at 38

behind my side of the headboard
my son sleeps with me
both eyes frozen open
his glass-housed body tap-taps against the wall
when I walk too hard through the room
with rushing morning feet
his face is a dandelion tree
and my windy sights blow on him each morning
seeds fly between us
and our love for each other lanterns the room
when I need to feel him close and mine
he burns wicked
and shy
while I sleep in a fetal curl
or make queensize love in a woman's pot of heat
he is so steadfast in his staring down
I am his cross to bear
when I need a word to finalize a line
that refuses my advances
he is always the teasing one
who raises his sweet voice
and keeps it away in the clouds
Mommy, you're not thinking deep enough
he has my ropey hair and spacey teeth
my love for precision
he keeps my same tentative smile all through the night
looking something and nothing like me all at once
but he is son to me
all the brown framed boy I have
Lobengula

the criss cross
between the men in my family
and those I loved early in my young woman's life
Everyday as he stares out
nailed high into his birth wall
I know I have missed ever knowing him
I have missed never marking his height off in the kitchen
or lip kissing his heart forever on the mitt of my hand
or smelling his sleeping high school breath for homemade wine
guzzled in the bus parking lot between quarters

"Who is that," wanderers to the bedroom ask.
"That is my son," I say. "He lives behind me there. He is a wallbound
     child."
"What is a wallbound child? And when did you have one?"
"It means if he leaves the air in this room he will die without me."
"But he is too big to still sleep with his mother. What would people say?"
"They would say I am unfit to have a son that can never leave his mother's
     room."

But they would be so wrong.

Fishing Among the Learned

On the banks of her butterfly pond
Grandmother would stand
as fluid as a waterfall
teaching with a Five and Dime pole in her hand

Be still, and listen to that
She could be heard to say

She would make
more good decisions
lose more control
gain and relinquish power
care about more people
recycle more energy
discern more foolishness
in an afternoon of Fishing
than Congress ever could
be they every one

unanimous
all Democrat
all Republican

My first semesters ever were spent
staring up at this Human University
shifting my weight from leg to leg
waving first cowfly then firefly from off her apron dress
and listening to the sound around us
there was noise there was instruction
there was indeed a difference in the two

This kind of standing stare at still water
this speaking on the depths of a true life lived full
Sociology
footprints baked into the soft bank
Geography Advanced
these outdoor lessons could go on for days
as long as there was sun and bait
there was learning

To educate means to lead out
she told me on the road home
I had no idea what she was saying or why now
At well lit nightfall
in between the quiver of country bugs I'd wonder
why does she stand me there each morning
that pole in my hands
gripped as tight as teeth full born to a jaw insisting
Pond water is as good as any book

A good teacher can do more than talk about it
She'd already said to me in dreams
She can see it clear

There on that bank
Preparing me for giant Orcas
when she knew full well in those days
Bream and Mullet were all we had tugging our lines

You don't fish just to catch
you fish so you can keep
so you can put something back

the teacher taught
it has less to do with the fish
and more to do with your line in the water
your hand on the pole
with discerning rituals
with what you can figure out about yourself
while standing there
in between the bites
know what you will not let corrupt you
that you cannot be bought or sold
assume another will come after you have long gone
their pole tight in hand as well
hoping to catch something
Put something back whenever you can

Now that is something to keep

I left her hot iron gates ready for labor
and the unforeseen anything in between

With a plain cane pole
Grandmother given
and a plastic bobber found
these days
I cast out among the Learned
and teach to alter sleeping states
I stand before the University Pond
and fish for the living
who bubble among the Learned
who know
real life bestows no terminal degrees

We all dangle here
caterpillars and grub worms
twirling into this new year
preparing one day for silk jackets
or sheepskin shoes for things better and days
deeper reasons
we cast out our many different lines
the baited and the barely hooked
the new recruits watch
the old sentries look out silent

as we push away from shore calling our rolls
like salmon remembering the way
do or die

I return too
determined that this year
fishing is the key
to everything
that moves

A poet needs to flyfish
sometimes
in the middle of the bluest grass
in order to catch glimpses of privileged information
that there are too many meetings
and not enough conversation going on
and stand girded before the listening eyes
of those who pay their hard earned money
to wonder if I am teaching anything
that the world will later ask of them
to be sure and know

I must

A poet needs to hope beyond hope
inside the polished granite of Academe
that the newly arrived
with their canes dragging in the sands will help
that others who have been here all along have not given up
that we all will keep going to the bank Fishing
but this time throwing our prime catch back
to forego the weigh-in of the dying
the comparison of scales
but keep the feeling of casting out close

I am Fishing to know that the Learned
are really hearing the living inside the walls and out
and not spending so much time and talk
just on our brilliant selves

A fishy poet invited to cast out a line
has to cast out a cat gut cord

a thousand pound live wire
with hook enough for all
and reel in everything she sees
and speak of the good with the bad and hope for the best
do or die

And for nine month cycles stand with the rest
spinning for silk for sheepskin for sanity
for something higher more enduring that sweet tenure or paper trails
for the sake of the high and honored art of teaching
of returning something real to the mental food chain
that of truthing to transform life

In the unnamed names of all the ghosted teacher women
soldiered around the edges of this pioneer groundscape
who for generations kept this place well oiled and honest
whose names go unexcavated still
I stand I cast I stare I feel I fish for what is true
so that the legacy of here is not what some of us believe
and others dare only whisper
that only men and horses and basketballs
make it to stone and get to last forever
that there is something here in these still waters
more powerful than we could ever imagine
it is something we have hooked but not yet pulled to surface
something we'll eternally feel on our lines but never lay our eyes upon
if we do not study the scholarship of Fishing

I am casting out a line to ensure
that our souls remain olive oiled and patient alive and able to hear
discern the noise from the instruction

A poetress sometimes must float in a beautiful man made pond
she must wade out among the Learned in order to learn
that none of us are casting far enough off shore
there in the dimpled uncharted waters
in the undiscovered raging sea
where more than what we expect always lives
and waits for the courageous to come and dip toe in
in the spirit of the old ones who would pull up anchor in a minute
and take their chances never worrying that all their eggs were in one
    basket

We have barricaded ourselves away
from the scholarship of risk from all the elements
that first made us feel and fight and therefore freely birth
conversation

This beginning together again is sacred ritual
and we remember
"If we do what we've always done,
we're gonna get what we've always gotten."

Don't pull your line in too fast
Grandmother would say out the corner of her eye.
Keep your gook in the water all the way to the edges,
that's where the great tadpoles swim.

There are possibilities all the way until the end
Whatever you do take Fishing with you
The sound of air bubbles and that of lips
pursed just below the surface of an idea ready to bite
and the bobber being pulled down right then
and once airborne and arcing the tiny mullet changing
to the giant Orca
right before our very Learned eyes

Now that is something to Keep

Ruth Forman

Ruth Forman, born in 1968, is a graduate film student at USC who has a specific interest in merging poetry and film. A student of June Jordan, Ishmael Reed, and Yusef Komunyakaa, her work has been anthologized in print and also featured on the PBS series The United States of Poetry. She received the 1992 Barnard New Women Poets Prize for her book We Are the Young Magicians.

This Poem

For Lisa

gonna be so slammin
dogs start barkin at nobody passin by
n everybody on Wall Street stop what they doin n say
damn
this poem gonna be so bad
lil girls don want no candy
lil boys hush n mamma don't get a headache
this poem gonna be so bad
daddy get home from work early
jus to dance wit mamma before dinner

this poem be barbecue hot hot hot n red cream soda
this poem be old jeans n new underwear
this poem be Cadillacs n ruby lips n goin out
this poem be curly curly hair
this poem be cowrie shells n kinte
this poem be Haitian dance n sage burnin
black black thick thick sweet sweet
n orange purple sunset when the car break down

this poem ride AC Transit
n this poem say a prayer for women n wheelchairs
alone at night
n this poem know you gave your lover alla you
n the thief won't give you back no pieces
but this poem say
girl your river's everflowin everlastin
so keep on steppin strong sister
this poem say God don love the repo man

n night sticks n broken ribs n bullet holes
in the left shoulder of a strong strong back

this poem be me talkin bout this poem be me talkin bout
your dog barkin
this poem be me talkin bout your lover laughin
talkin bout you talkin bout you in this poem
be you laughin you black you thick
you sweet sweet honey on my pancakes in the mornin
sunrise in your fingers singing
what this poem gonna be
n i don care if i sound like um stuck in the sixties
this poem slammin this poem black
n nobody tell me nothin cuz i said it
this poem be us n
this poem be poetry

Waitin on Summer

Daddy
is hot butter corn bread in the winter
n a big size 44 belt
chasin me round the kitchen table

Daddy
is thunder with the brothers
light rain with the sisters
n lightning with me n Richie
if we dance on the living room floor

Daddy
is smooth blue sky
in his Sedan de Ville
on Sunday afternoon

Daddy
is hot butter corn bread in the winter
pork n beans n boiled hot dogs
but when the thermometer hit 75
n it's time to barbecue
n times is good
n me n Richie don't run in the house

Daddy
is cool cool lemonade
with the peel
jus floatin on top

Green Boots n Lil Honeys

n i'm waitin for the light to turn green/
n i see these two fat kentucky fried oozie-lookin brothas/
peepin me like i'm the lil cutie/wantin to jump in
their long Sanford n Son lookin hooptie/
now i'm not one to judge or nothin/
but these two look like the kind who might/
give me a free flight into the wall/
jus cuz i'm not actin right/if you know what i mean
n they smilin at me/n i'm waitin for the light to turn green
n tryin to look like i'm real into the sidewalk/
cuz that's where it's at/n i can feel these brothas
jus waitin for me to hop into the back seat/
where the springs poppin out/all the time
i'm thinkin/why these folks lookin
like i want to get with them so bad

n all the time i'm thinkin of the videos
you know/where the brotha's in the beat up car/
drivin real slow/he got money/
but he don't put it into his car/
cuz Oakland Police stop him twice as many times a night
if he had somethin like a BMW/cuz they know
if he got a dope car he a dope dealer/
anyway/it's kinda makin sense now/
cuz it's kinda in style for lil honeys
to be all over somebody big who look like
somethin white people call the police on
cuz they jus look wrong/
n honeys be all over them in like twos n threes
sometimes/in the videos/i know you seen them/
so what i'm sayin is it's kinda in style to be kissin
n huggin n rubbin on somebody
who knock you out in a minute/
but still give you money to get ya nails done/
it's hip you know/in style n shit/

n i'm not one who don't like style
cuz i'm lookin kinda fly
in my knee green boots and black raiders jacket/
but you know style ain't what you see on tv

n all the time these brothas think imma get with them/
cuz they the B-boys/n they been gettin some play/
n they been thinkin they can get some more
from this here honey on the corner/well
i'm jus not that much in style

n the light turns green n they cruise by real slow/
makin sure i get a good look
at em/but you know the sidewalk is what's happenin/
i told you that already/
i pretend i don't see em but i shoulda screamed on em/
SEE YOU IN THE VIDEOS/ that i turn on when i'm tired
of lookin at that damn news/you know/
where war is kinda in style/
green boots n gas masks/ you know/
how in high school the recruiter rolls by/
talkin bout how you can earn money/
get a education/see the world/n people hop in cuz
these folks tryin to get where they goin/ wherever that is/
n they seen on tv that it's kinda in style to hop on over
to somethin that will fuck you up in a minute/
n they didn't really know it would be like that/
trying to find a way out from where they're at/
n somebody drive by offerin all this kinda shit/
n they think it's kinda cool cuz you know/
on tv it's kinda cool to be a soldier/kinda in style/
n the big dealers just sittin up there/
thinkin you be their lil honey
or somethin/n i wonder why
they think i be down for somethin like that/ why
we be down for somethin like that/
n i think it's cuz it's in style or somethin
like biker shorts n gold teeth n Ray Bans
to cover a black eye/
everybody seem like they down for alla that
cuz nobody say nothin different/
n i don't neither/i jus keep on waitin on the green light

You So Woman

For Anya

lady
when ya purple heels hit concrete
afros swing
cool jazz hot baby
strollin by cry amen

so holy
preachas stutta
thighs so righteous
pews jump up n catch the spirit n
hymns speak in tongues

so sweet
bees leave the daffodils behind
for honey you make table sugar taste sour n
Mrs. Butterworth sho can't find a damn thing to say
when you aroun

lookin so good
cockroaches ask you to step on em
sos they can see heaven
befo
and after they die n

you love ya people so much
if you was on pilgrimage
the Sahara Desert would run to the Atlantic
jus to make sure you don't get thirsty n
camels would kiss you for choosin they back

but Africa don't got you
we do n glad too

so girl
you jus keep on
makin the sunset procrastinate n
givin the rainbows a complex
you a silk earthquake

you a velvet hurricane
n girl you so woman
i be damn
if you don't put a full moon to shame.

Brian Gilmore

Brian Gilmore, born in 1962, is a writer, poet, and attorney based in Washington, D.C. His publications include work in Obsidian II, The Washington Afro-American, *and* The Nation. *His first collection of poetry,* elvis presley is alive and well and living in harlem, *was published in 1993.*

revolution
for my father, wilmer i. gilmore

my father was a dictator.
in 1968 dad suspended the house
constitution
instituted a state of emergency
suspended any rights that television
made us think we had
he declared tarzan a fake
nat turner ·important
malcolm x a brother that
we must understand.

it was strange this regime;
it promulgated propaganda about
the importance of reading books
the danger of always watching television
and how
being black was the coolest thing
you could ever know.

often my brother and i rebelled against
this totalitarian despot,
we declared civil war by
staying out on the streets until 4 or 5 a.m.
all the time.
el presidente would be awake
always when we returned.
calm in his demeanor, he greeted us with
one of those well prepared 4-hour speeches like
fidel castro. this constant pounding
on our brains made us

surrender eventually and end our unrest after
nearly 20 years of disorganized resistance.
the will of this monarch
became our will:
like, you will go to school
you will not fuck up your life.

now when i stop by my father's house
the state of emergency is over
the revolution he declared was successful
the laws he passed are no longer in need
of enforcement

these presidential duties are exclusively mine now
and if
i am ever so lucky to become
a dictator
i shall not hesitate
to "dis"
tarzan and give really long
speeches
in
another language.

to be or not to be . . .

ACT I
polonius is still alive.
rosencranz is still spying.
guildenstern is taking pictures of
all the niggahs thinking. thinking
and waiting until the ghost returns.

returns with the news of our end,
in a place that reminds me of denmark
and looks like america,
or is it a place that reminds me of america
and looks
like
south afrika?

ACT II

the king has banged our momma. the king has killed
our daddy. the king with
            the ship
            and the quest for
            gold.
            the king with guns and powder
            and daddy with the spear that's broken

we are reciting soliloquies and forever
loving our uncle.

ACT III

"there is something rotten in denmark . . ."
something old
re-written
and performed
at too many theatres.

denmark is unsafe for spooks.

ACT IV

malcolm was mad. dr. king was mad.
garvey
nat t
fred d
were all mad.
there is method to their madness,
says the king.
they did not think,
thinkers read soliloquies and slowly become
yorick.

ACT V

we are hamlet. we were warned by
our fathers.
there are too many poison cups
too many poison swords
too many niggahs
behind the curtain with polonius.

the king is banging our momma
and killing our daddy
and we recite soliloquies
and defy the visit
of the ghost.

coming to the net
for arthur ashe

now we must come to the net,
with our rackets
our skills;
rushing the net
ready for the lob that our
opponent always seems to rely on.
ready to slam the shot into the
open court,
that's all we need now is an opening,
a clear chance to take control
of this match,
a double fault
an unforced error
a slow high bouncing return that we can handle,
send back with violent force,
drive our opponent into the fence so
we can come to the net for the shot
that will make history.

now we must prepare our rackets;
back behind us and ready,
we just need to keep the ball in
play now,
it is match point but we must have the heart
of a champion.
we must all be in grand slam form.
wimbledon
the french
the u.s. open
it might be match point
but this is how greatness is born.

now we must be ready to serve.
a hard driving
up in your face
roscoe tanner look alike.
pushing our opponent
back against the fence
telling him we will
not be beat.
we can then come to the net
with our rackets prepared
ready for the lob
checking down the line
determined to turn this thing
around
because all we need is an opening,
and i know we can be victorious,
if we all come to the net together.

gas station attendant
for ms. haywood

"... *running on empty* ... "
Jackson Browne

when she and i
do not talk
i am like my car running on
empty
the fumes of our last
conversation push me
down the lonely desolate
highway looking anxiously
for a sign
that says
i can

fill up again

the car i drive is a gas guzzling
mid sized heap that would
benefit from a 24-hour self service
station right next to my house

i have plans to
build a station there myself and hire
a one person
staff

i hope she doesn't mind
the demanding
work schedule

Keith Gilyard

Keith Gilyard, born in 1952 and raised in New York City, is on the faculty of Syracuse University. His work in several genres has appeared in many magazines, journals, and anthologies. His volume of poetry, American Forty, *was published in 1993. Gilyard received an American Book Award for his 1991 book of memoir and essays,* Voices of the Self.

Daughter, That Picture of You
For Kaamilah

after they sawed through the bone
in your thorax
to close the hole
in your heart
that would not
for four years
despite what experts said
close itself
they scalpeled you
sutured you
into a stranger
half alive

hooked you to
the ominous respirator
and wheeled you back up
to intensive care

almost helpless
a waxed warrior
draped in tape
and tubes
up your nose
down your throat
in your chest
in your arm
legs
mine trembling
as i make the standard silent promise

(i can't keep)
not to be impatient
ever again

fear rooted
in my legs
fear ruling
my fingers
fear riding
my voice
as i ask
if
after all this
you could still smile for daddy

and you did

Portraits of a Moment

my hands ooze over you
as the warm slow bottle of lotion
your skin aches for

we enrich
the language of tender moanings
and stretch the kiss
like Bird stretched music

i sip of the joy
in your eyes
and they capture me:
your eyes, like the sun,
already as constant and good
as they must be
and just as the sun
please eyes like the sun
rise always

oh how your fingers need!
and i have become the harp
you play so gently

i offer lyrics to hang around our necks
like matching sets of beads.

Letter

from what i've been hearing
you're doing allright
you may not realize it
but your the only one
doing something constructive
out of all the people
i grew up with

so please for me
keep it up
and don't let the oppression of this society
stop you

i feel i can be capable of strugle
too
so far i haven't did so good
but now i'm moving
and your acheevements help me along

all people who are part of the strugle
help me to be strong
but you mean more
because of what we went thru
together

this jail sentence
is gonna be longer
than all the others
put together
i'll get at lease
10 of the possible 25

the racist m.f. judge told me
i shoulda been stealing
welfare checks because
arm bank robbery is very
distasteful

you get his drift
don't be fucking around
with the power structure
strike the people
of your community

i told him he
could kiss my ass
racist punk

i didn't realize how much
of a degenerate society
amerika is until i got
in federal authority's
hands

i got a lot more
to rap to you about
but have to go
now

so write back
i want to keep
intouch

remember
make sure you write

On Top of It All

get on top
no, not that old sex position
the renewed search for the magic
of an imploding star

get on top
no, not a frenzied scramble
up the soul killing rungs
of a corporate ladder

but on top like elvin jones atop the cymbals
splashing news down the mouth of music

elvin on the i.d.
inside the stomach like a gastroscope
drumstick light on disease
then trane on top with the surgery
saxophonic scalpel slicing the gut of boredom

and then all of that the drum
the drum is the drum
the saxophone is the drum
malcolm resolve is the piano
race space the bass
self-the-horn (that's you)
self-the-horn on top of that

build the solo
build the solo

riffs of memory

a day no longer than a peanut butter & jelly sandwich
a story no bigger than your intrigue
a meadow no more innocent than your questions

build the solo
build the solo

a clone of sadness stuck in misery's back alley
plucking harsh chords on the ghetto's silent harp
the misdirected medicine man called a dope dealer
blood running like ketchup down a brown snow forearm
all the blue men dreaming of red wine
all the blue men dreaming of all wine
whipped women are vain warnings
superimposed upon daughters smiling
like optimistic beacons holding
joys too vast to give view
of hazards to be run and
battles to be lost
and whipped women are vain warnings
a barefoot hippie asking you
to sign his prayer book on the #7 train

build the solo
build the solo

weaving the patchwork of hard pressing
and soft lazy kisses
all around the beautiful women of fantasy
the holding of unreality in your arms
the only almost satisfied feeling
the bye bye signs wrapped around the aortas
of the women who would see them when they searched inside
others who said farewell all too well for your ego
the strangers who gazed at you through a periscope
as you danced the floors of la martinique
the hustle
the bump
the rub but you were cool

build the solo
build the solo

the neighborhood party you can't have
who can r.s.v.p. from the graveyard?
not duck
not dobie
not jerome
not genie
not gunner
not stoney
not larry (neither one)
not rube
not stevie
not gene (neither one)
not even gene's son
not danny
not reggie
not douglas (neither one)
not joker
not freddie
not shy (neither one)
not breadhead
not ivan
not dwight
not travis
not ronnie (neither one)
not marcus
not bobby
not derrick

not chicago
not keno
not t.k.

no special guest appearance by marvin gaye

then all of that the drum
the memory is the drum
the world is the drum
lovers gouging out each other's hearts with mutual love
children with other meanings to fire to life
poets with not enough lines
death is the drum

and you're out and on top
the planets the keyboard
the sun the bass
and self-the-horn (that's you)
self-the-horn to the top of the universe

a lyrical potion of privileged forever
and you're right here all the time
and be gone
present day licks as quick and definite as air rushing out
the behind of an untied balloon set in flight
and be gone
on top of it all
and gone

Daniel Gray-Kontar

Daniel Gray-Kontar, born in 1971, is a student and writer from Cleveland, Ohio. A senior at Cleveland State University, he has performed his work for large audiences across the nation and is featured on the sound recording The Best of the National Poetry Slam, Volume One.

cuz' mama played jazz

when i was six years old
mama played the first song
on the first side
of an album with the illustration
of a Black man on the cover
by hisself
with a short haircut
and a closed left fist on the left side of his face.

she played that song whenever uncle joe and aunt yvette came over,
or when skinny dudes with fat afros and blue sunglasses
invaded our living room
saying things like:

"yeah, that jimmy carter got a knife in his back,"
or
"that danny green shit that went down wasnt even cool,"
or
"what the fuck ever happened between miriam and rahsheeed?"
or
"go out in the bush, fuck wit' dem lions,"
(imitating richard pryor jokes).

mama would play that tune
whenever she was in a good mood,
and one time, when i had come into the house
after a long day up the block,
she told me what the name of it was.

"you remember that song that we sang together
when we watched that movie, 'the sound of music'?"
she asked.

then she'd catch up with the melody and sing:
"brown paper packages tied up with string,
these are a few of my favorite things."

her voice danced with the piano notes
that gently pulled her shy soprano into the air
as the two swayed together
rhythmically.
methodically.
beautifully.
"yeah, i guess i remember,"
i said.
but honestly, i only remembered the song as
the first groove
on the first side
of the album with the man on the cover
by hisself
with the short haircut.

cuz' mama played jazz,
i listened.

when i was twelve years old,
mama played donald byrd.

do, do, do (click, click)
do.
        do.

it was mama sitting in another living room
still listenin to that jazz.

what was it that mama heard in those notes
that made her sit in that room
nodding her head back and forth,
eyes closed
perfectly content in her solitude?

i sure didnt know.
but she listened on
and on
and on . . .

until one day,
i finally heard
what she heard.

she heard the music talkin.
she heard the music talkin the way we be talkin.

when that byrd was on,
it was as though mama were listenin in
on a conversation
in her imagination.

so
cuz' mama played jazz,
i listened.
and
cuz' mama played jazz
i write.
and now
i just fill in what the music said
inside my head.

scubee doo day,
da doo dah,
doo wow.

not no socialism/communism classical, but some power to the people jazz

rilly,
im a brown man.
but they got we callin we
Black
and we dont even know that we aint
Black.
and they got we callin we
Black
when we all rilly
African.

they got us callin them
White
and got some of them callin each other
White.
and they aint rilly white-
they pink
(or somethin like that).

funny how they
wanna keep us all
mixed up like that.

Black is objective.
White is too.
But pink and brown
ain't quite so simple.
you cant put pink against brown
like you can put Black against White.
makin shit blackandwhite
means having to choose sides
between blackandwhite.

but i'll tell you what blackandwhite is.

i'll tell you what blackandwhite is.

black is capitalism.
white is capitalist.
black is imperialism
white is imperialist.
black is racism.
white is racist.
black is right.
white is wrong.
black is wrong.
white is right.
white is today.
black is tonight.

black is white is/ black is white is/ black is white is/ white is black/
is white is black/ is white black?/ is white black?/ is white black?/
is white is black is white is black is

outta sight is out of
mind
is you
out of your blackandwhite mind?

its time that brown and pink
got together
and found out what blackandwhite
rilly is.

its time that pink and brown
got together
and found out what blackandwhite
rilly is.

and after we found out
then
pink can be pink
and brown can be brown.
pink can be pink and
brown can be brown.

if you didnt know that rodney king
was black
youda kept on burnin.
if you didnt know that coon
was white
youda never stopped lootin
would never stopped lootin
its yours anyway,
take it nigga/brown, brown nigga/
take it cracka/pink, pink cracka/
and let em know who took it.
tell em
the niggas took it
tell em
the crackas took it
tell em
the spics took it
tell em
the spades/ the moulies/ the coons/ the honkies/ the poor white trash/
the wops/the dagos/the gooks/the nuyoricans and inner city ricans/
took it

tell em
you took the truth when you took that tv,
you looted the truth when you looted that loveseat
picked up the truth and carried it on your shoulders,
placed it in purses,
paraded it up the street
and proudly put it in pickup trucks—
placed it in piles
took it for miles.

tell em that
pink and brown took the truth
and found out that the truth aint always

blackandwhite
is black is white is/ black is white is/ black is white
is
White
rilly
Black?

well. that would be another story
all together, now.
wouldnt it?

july

> your tune is a tempest of heat
> with an arrangement of rain seductively sweet.
> your arrival awakens mother instinct
> while brothers, standing on corners
> philosophizing and shooting the shit
> simultaneously shoot sharp glances
> at officers of the fifth precinct
> as they roll by
>
> summer is july.
>
> can you hear
> the mighty rumble of heat thunder
> as we eye our enemy
> in this concrete jungle?

july is rebellion.

for if the spring of life is april
and a time of birth,
then july is adolescence.
a time when one learns of
the abstract
according to piaget

so its only natural that the rebellious
rise in the next day.

july is revolution.
july is summer.
cant you
hear
the drummer?

Duriel Harris

Duriel Harris was born in 1969 and is originally from Chicago. She moved to New York to pursue a degree in creative writing at NYU. She teaches high school English at the Dalton School in Manhattan.

For My Father

December/ no signs of a Chicago winter/ no boulder-sized clumps of snow/ patches of dirty ice/ stalled or snowed-in rust-stuck cars/ it was nippy/ I started to walk the two blocks home/ because my father was running
     Saturday
errands with the car/ I veered right towards McDonald's/ the balding
     greying
brown head that I saw bent-necked over a table of newspapers seemed
familiar/ it was my father/ stopped for a cup of noon coffee/ black and
     bitter/
with his three papers before he returned home from the dry cleaners/ the
leather man/ Pete's Produce/ a moment of solitude/ anonymity

No one was to open the newspaper before my father did/ especially not the comics/ none of us could seem to re-fold the pages correctly/ we destroyed newspaper neatness/ misplaced the creases

I saw him/ the shape of a man fit into the yellow plastic trunk of a swivel
chair/ he didn't look up/ I thought about his weekend casuals/ slightly
     faded
relaxed fit Levi's jeans and Reebok walking shoes/ I imagined my father on
the way to work/ everyday/ 6:15 am/ the side-to-side rocking walk/ short
     tan
trenchcoat/ briefcase/ dark suit/ cuffs/ wing tips stern and sexy/ climbing
the steps of the 87th Street bus or the #14/ with a fresh Sun-Times nooked
     in
his right armpit/ often to return/ at 9 or 10 pm/ from the office/ bible
     study/
board meetings/ choir rehearsal/ church council/ Sundays/ two services and counting money afterward

When I was little/ and Daddy was in town/ I still might not see him for 3
     or 4

days/ late to bed/ early to rise/ the goodbye kiss roused me from sleep/ My
high school years we left together/ When my morning was slow/ he
 would
wait/ fully dressed/ then leave/ looking back/ I'd run to catch up/ as he
 stood
calmly/ shaking his head/ Does he know that I am watching him/ from the
other side of the glass?

my father/ could be just another old man/ his roundness/ dark brown
 narrow
eyes/ behind bifocals/ dimming with the yellow glaze of age/ thin grey
moustache/ shave-burned face/ reading/ alone/ neither special nor
s i g n i f i c a n t

I love this man who calls himself ugly/ painfully aware of his
 awkwardness/
small but indelicate failures/ elegant and human in the knowing

Landscapes

The afternoon sun/ somewhere in the South

Year 1910: On the shaded side steps of Centennial Baptist Church in
 Helena/
where Crowley's Ridge and the Mississippi meet/ almost touch/ a woman
 stops/
fingers a black shawl/ looks out/ To steady herself she leans on the railing/
sings a whisper:
I tole Jesus
that it would be alright
if he changed my name

Douglass said Lloyd's Ned/ Morrison said Macon Dead and Sing
talking drums say the people could fly
the griot/ general store porchlight storyteller/ weeknight and all day
 Sunday
preacher/ shape cypress knees/ talk about the gang/ box and pullman cars/
cuz every story this century has a train

Listen: hisses like steam heat hisses like engines/ Stimela/ the weight of
 cargo
shifting/ breathing/

Hugh Masekela plays the trumpet live
mimics the music of the coal train destined for Johannesburg
eeeeeeekk tchtch tchtch tchtch sssssssshhhhh
His mouth makes steam sounds/ spits sweat
For every story this century has a train:
unmarked train/ coal train/ freedom train
cain't hand paddle up the Mississippi
Railroad moves 'em North past/ high water marks on Delta trees

All Memory of the land: rice/ cotton/ soy/ red-clay clinging dust like snuff/
pinched in the spaces between the flat planks of the "H" and "I"/ a strand
     of
feathers/ barely visible/ trailing soft behind the "O"/ CHICAGO/ city of
onions/ trading post of Jean Baptiste Point-DuSable/ headlined promised
     land
in the North . . .

Blues City/ Gangster City/ Windy City of many churches/ liquor stores and
lounges/ big city juke joints like junkyard litter on the West and South
     Sides/
the black-hand side up under the El tracks jack/ with a stash of smack cat
d a d d y / y e a h h h Hip-hop is be-bop in another language

Year 1995:
same landscape/ same game/ cards cut with even teeth and a little sugar/ a
leaf-less shade tree by the storefront/ salt-cracked buckled sidewalks/ the
     hiss
and clank of heat rising through rusting pipes/ the hawk darting quick
through the just-opened door/ a woman stops on the single step/ shudders/
her eyes water from the cold

on the uptown lexington avenue express:
Martin Luther King Day 1995

This morning/ there is a woman giving a sermon/ Her voice trembles
     over the
heads of the standing passengers/ impatiently checking their watches/
lurching forward & back/ with every stutter/ stall/ screeching halt/ false
start/ Her voice hovers near the ceiling/ then comes down/ manna/ dust
settling on the rows of nodding heads that line the car

She speaks of growing up in the sixties/ what was in America/ a decade of
change and turmoil/ hope/ when the air was tangible/ a tight lightness of
atoms/ bodies that traveled in the current/ the movement/ displaced the
     air/
when everything was metal against metal/ when everything was a dirge or
shout or silence

Divine providence/ that she came to know the ways of the Lord Jesus/
     p r a i s e
God/ the Living God/ a wheel in the middle of a wheel/ the train snug in
     its
track/ from Atlantic Avenue to 42nd Street/ the man standing next to her
     has
an inner balance/ reads his newspaper/ drinks steaming coffee/ is a stone

Conversations are few/ this morning/ just the woman's sermon/ and the
     roar
of the train/ a call and response/ lulling the rush-hour crowd/ smashed
     black
and white together/ a mass of bodies/ and briefcases/ eyes closed or pasted
f o r w a r d

I stand next to the man/ next to the preaching woman/ by the door/ I focus
     my
eyes/ behind the woman whose seat I want

Fannie Lou Hamer stares back/ through poster printed words: "I'm sick
     and
tired of being sick and tired. We gonna fight for freedom."/ her words cut
something in me/ I am in some other time/ the people and the train
disappear/ there is only the sound of movement/ and a soft milky
     whiteness/
smooth biscuit-dough light

Divine Providence/ and the Lord don't care 'bout your color/ Praise God/
     said
the Lord knows your heart and your struggles/ Praise the Lord/ and ain't
     no
freedom in this world like the freedom of the kingdom of the living God

I focus my eyes/ as if seeing is understanding/ pictures of dogs and hoses
turned upon children/ clips of newsreels/ marching and picketing/ and

sitting and standing/ and fire and bombings/ and gun shots/ bricks/ blows/
singing and shouting/ the silent sway of bodies on gnarled trees/ all in
        grainy
black and white/ The blood is grey in the pictures/ the Klan/ hooded sheets
and crosses/ marching in Chicago/ Marquette Park/ commemoration of the
first Holiday

and there/ splitting her face/ a ragged stretch across the poster/ Sweaty Will
has scratched his tag and response/ with a black finepoint pen: "nice
        quote.
now pick cotton bitch"

I am back in New York/ on the uptown lexington avenue express/ I want
        to get
off the train/ or scream/ but the doors and my throat are closed

what we have lost

can you hear it/ a *faint echo/ vespers from the book of ancestry/ once
        bound*
& sealed/ melismata/ catalysts for the slow backward wind

fashioned/ blood, tooth & bone/ from earth/ we now stand erect/ evolved
        from
the cell/ vestiges of what was before/ residue/ like oil on the fingers/ or a
        lingering sourness/ familiar
& elusive

something is falling/ I try to remember what it was like before/ I was a
        little
girl once/ my body a smooth board of flesh

I see her in family photographs/ wearing mother's hats/ she was always
smiling/ for the camera/ loved taking pictures/ loved men & daddy's winter
wing tips/ loved men & their long-muscled laps

it was there she played/ her favorite game with daddy/ trapped in the
        nooks of
his arms/ "gotcha" he would say/ "you'll never get away"/ one quick
        wiggle/ a
squirm/ & poof!/ she would escape

delight roasting in almond eyes to see daddy/ grin/ searching the space
where she had been/ one blind hand stirring the pot/ "where did she go?"

I was a little girl once/ I see her in family photographs/ smiling & laughing
with the men and lanky boys/ unguarded/ her arms swing/ she fills the
      frame

I pass my hands over my breasts/ the hair damp between my legs/ my sex/
      the
soft sponge of my buttocks/ it is dark because my eyes are closed/ I am
      small/
the air a swathe of cotton/ I am still/ I feel them moving their bodies
      through
me/ into the mattress/ the floor/ the wall behind me/ my lips brushed with
sweat salt/ I taste them in my ears/ the air is thick with their pounding/ the
sea/ the river/ my skin/ wet & slick/ feverish/ separates into molecules/
      all of
the blood to the surface/ to the surface

there were years in between

I was a little girl once/ I want to speak this into being/ soft skull &
      gristle/
fallen into the world/ before I could know to fear/ to flee/ before I could
recognize the act/ name it and its owners/ push them out of me/ through
      the
mirror/ Now we are one flesh that knows no boundaries

memory-traces/ white wisps of chalk dust on a child's wiped slate/ standing
again before the glass/ who can be certain/ what we have lost/ is worth
calling back

Safiya Henderson-Holmes

Safiya Henderson-Holmes, born in 1952, is an associate professor in the Creative Writing Program at Syracuse University. A writer of fiction and poetry, she is author of Madness and a Bit of Hope, *which received the Poetry Society of America's William Carlos Williams award, and* Daily Bread. *Her poems appear in numerous anthologies, textbooks, and periodicals. She dedicates this inclusion to her father Chet Otis Lee Henderson.*

"C" ing in Colors: Red

"There once was a girl
with a curl in the middle
of her forehead. When she was good
she was very, very good.
But when she was bad
she was horrid."

1.
I don't remember being very, very good or horrid. But I do remember the wish for curls dangling from my forehead; long, silky, slinky curls over my shoulders, that windblowin, hangover the pillow stuff, the moviestar, made-in-America and on T.V. stuff. Perhaps the horrid came with the realization of the curls' absence. Perhaps the very, very good came with the hope that with enough pulling and greasing and straightening and do-rag praying the curls would soon appear and I'd be . . .

2.
A dread instead.
I'm a dark brown girl with my father's southern, determined, been black and back hair. The stuff meteorologists predict the weather with, the call and response, hallelujah stuff. My mother has the "other" colored hair, the mixed goods. I'd comb my mother's hair as she slept, comb it gently across her pillow into lay-flat, do-right styles as we both dreamed. Some nights I combed until . . .

3.
I'm bald. I'm not hip-hop, be-bop, rap, reggae, funk, cool, singed by lightning, making a religious, or an enlightened statement. I'm not

trying to impress or address a living soul. I'm standing before myself and the many mirrors, in whatever room a woman has ever walked, ran or stood in. The rapunzel issue is still on, ever growing, but not growing on my head, or under my arms, or over my "way-down-there" place, or over my eyes.

4.

The black woman hair issue is blood hot: dreadlocks, braids, weaves, wigs, blonde, brown, jetblack, not very often gray, even when bald, it has to be a cool bald, you know, like you go to a barber and say, "f——, cut it all off, liberation bald, solidarity bold, bald. But . . .

5.

I'm twenty five pounds less, nauseous, dizzy. The veins in my arms are lit matches under my skin. I'm afraid of sleeping, afraid of waking. The friends and family around me, however close are on another side. Some days I can't even see them. Food sucks. Water, a miracle of blandness. It's Nov. 22nd 1994, 7:30am, my daughter's on her way to school, the doorbell rings, my friend's on time, she's going with me to the barber. I'm cutting my hair, my dreadlocks of eleven years. I cut my hair as a challenge, as a dare. I dare you Cytoxin, Platinol, Adrimycin, Pregnisone. I dare you to take a strand of this nappy hair before I do. And yes I know yall's stories of dead hair on the pillow, dead hair on the shower floor, dead hair in the lover's hand. Yall bad, some of the baddest drugs on the market. This is chemotherapy. It can kill, it can cure, but it cannot have my dreadlocks.

6.

I do, in a plastic bag in my closet, my barber has a lock, my friend has a lock. I haven't seen the skin of my scalp since birth, neither has the sun, or my daughter, or my mother, or my lover. I feel as though I'm before a mirror for the first time in my life, looking like E.T. looking like a victim of some undefined and undeclared war, not looking like anyone I know, or have a name for, looking fetal and painfully pure. What to do? What's the baby's response after birth, after being slapped into life? The tears, visible and invisible roll on for days. My head's cold. Hats, an admission of something going wrong. I rub my bald head for luck, for love. I want to be brave. I want to be beautiful. I want to be . . .

7.

A poem. But not a poem about tumors. I want to be a story. But not a word about pain. I want to be a performance piece. But not one utterance about the "C" word. I can't write. I won't write. But then how to create myself out of this unknown self? What to create with this bare head and bare heart. My lover says I'm beautiful. But he's away. His touch charges in from the distance. Sometimes

8.
his touch is too much, sometimes it's not enough. Sometimes we both hold on for dear life. My daughter is watching me die and live at the same time. Even while watching T.V., even while playing with her cats, she watches me fall and stand. It angers and frightens her. She leaves herself all over the house "a crumb trail" for the mommy she knows, for the mommy she needs. This is chemo. This is me. This is

9.
January 1995. My fourth month of chemotherapy. I make no new year resolutions, but I do pray, hope, wish, make a toast to that funny looking woman in the mirror, still nameless and bald. Sometimes when I'm alone with her in the bathroom mirror I trace her scars with my fingers. She seems to like that. She smiles, arcs her arms over her head, pirouettes. Lately, she's been saying we have to talk. I don't . . .

10.
know the time or day when it happened, but it happened.
I don't remember sitting, standing, in the infusion room, or in my bathtub. But I do remember feeling it when it happened. It was as if I was being scrubbed from head to toe with a soft brush. As if every centimeter of me was being cleared, removed of everything except air, except light. I remember holding my hands to my face and feeling wet, not tears, not bathwater. Sweat.

11.
Not the nightsweats doctors spoke of, or a cold sweat. It was a body wringing out. A body running a marathon, crossing a finish line. What Happened?

12.
I decided to go shopping. Yes shopping. I wanted to buy something new, something preciously new and alluring. Something long and lacey, racey. Something red and alarmingly low. I

13.
wanted to seduce myself. I wanted to attract myself to that mirror, to that nameless woman. I wanted to step, wanted to strut, to sashay

towards her all done-up and new. Then, maybe I'd take her out and love her to pieces, or love her whole. I

14.
felt silly with this feeling, I felt full. Even as Cytoxin flowed I felt whimsical. I bought a red dress.

15.
Short, fitting my hips just-so, for work, for play. On sale.
I bought a teal, twirling, gold buttons tapping down the front,
dancing dress, with pockets of course. I bought a knit turquoise skirt,
long with matching kimono sweater, too gorgeous to leave in store.
Not on sale.

16.
Breathless. I bought an "i have arrived" winter-white, tuxedo and a please look and touch, cream in your dreams, black lace body suit.
I bought shoes, boots, underwear, perfume. I spent some kind of money on "things" I had never bought for myself before.

17.
No, not things, on "ideas" I never considered for my-self before. I didn't own a red dress, never such a color for winter. My wardrobe functioned like a well behaved child. I had "good" clothes, not "bad" clothes. I dare not. I

18.
thought I wasn't shapely enough for "bad" clothes, those cling and pull-it-to-me clothes, I thought my shyness wouldn't allow sexy, that my feminism didn't call for lace. Nauseous and trembling I

19.
brought my new clothes home. I was home alone. I carried the bags into the bathroom, closed the door. I didn't look into the mirror until I was naked, old clothes on the toilet seat. I saw the "other" woman standing as ever, bald. Reluctantly, we pirouetted together, our knees and ankles weak. I stared her dead in the eyes, whispered "me". We cried, banged our darkened by chemo fingertips on the mirror. She wanted out. I

20.
dressed in the cream in your dreams black lace body suit,

21.
posed in every angle for her, for me. Bald heads gleaming under the
bathroom lights. I sprayed the bathroom with the new perfume. Me
and I laughed. We were so beautiful. We were so sweet.

22.
We are so beautiful. We are so sweet. I said to Me, weird how we had
to get stripped of everything to become beautiful, to accept ourselves
with ourselves, with or without what we know as pretty, as enough,
as sexy. Weird how it is that we stand here now, before ourselves
with less of ourselves, but somehow with much more.

23.
Me said, we're not talking clothes. I said, I know. Me said, but we
look damn good.

24.
Me and I don't have many parties or grand events to go to these
days, and these nights don't have much sex. But when Me and I go to
the doctors, the clinics, get x-rayed, blood tested, buy groceries we
are dressed to the eye-teeth, and at night we hold on to ourselves.
Sometimes in seductive lingerie, Sometimes in seductive nothing.
We've come to the very common realization that every extra day
given is a grand, and rare event, a time for dress-up, a time to have
it going on, and being all of that and a bag of chips. Even when you're
head to toe bald because of the "C"

25.
Word.

26.
We wear our beads.
We wear our feathers.
We wear our skin.

"C" ing in Colors: Blue

It was fall, early in the morning.
It is fall, early in the morning.
Things turn.

1.
October 31st 1994 7:30 am, on a street in Syracuse New York I'm a
black female disguised as a scary bag of bones. In my right lung I
carry a Jack-O-Lantern which surgery couldn't carve. I enter a

Hematology, Oncology clinic. A haunted house. I walk slowly towards the infusion area. There are monsters.

2.
October 16th 1995 early in the morning, rallying against monstrosities of racism and beasts which dwell in their own souls, a million black men dressed in the bewitching costumes of atoned skin, faces unmasked, hands empty arrive in Washington D.C. on buses, trains, cars, planes, long walks, leaving work, leaving cardboard covered benches. They've been arriving for days.

3.
The Million Man March on Washington D.C. and my follow up doctor's appointment to check on the size of Jack had been planned for months. October 16th is x-ed in every calendar I own. The day is Monday, a moon or lunar day. The day's color is blue for spirit or air. The number's seven for luck or change. The news media follows the men to D.C. I go alone to the doctor. We are in the armor and amour of skin.

4.
Infusion: (trick or treat) to infuse, to instill, inculcate, to steep or soak without boiling. (There's no safe candy here)

5.
Every haunted house I've ever been in is the same to me. Distorted lights and angles of floors, cries in walls, faces and hands reaching, falling into and out of darkened places, darkened places around corners, corners slippery and cold.

6.
And there's always a door that seems to dare me, "the spooked one" to open or close it. I breathe, hold my breath. When I've summoned the courage to grab the handle, because I know it's halloween and only the candy's real; a monster leaps, takes my tongue and I run, eyes closed somewhere.

7.
I strip for the doctor. The room's cold, corners slippery. The doctor listens to my lungs, surveys my radiation burned back and suture creased chest. Who but a doctor's eye to show such skin to, who but a doctor's touch? I think of the black men in Washington D.C. The doctor looks at my chart. I look at my breast. The quiet, almost shy scar above the right. I imagine the men.

8.
I imagine the brothers, fathers, sons, bringing their sons, fathers,
brothers, bringing pictures of dead homies in their wallets and
hearts, bringing their hearts on their sleeves like women, their
hearts on t-shirts like girls. Grown men in special haircuts and a
Sundays' best or whatever's left over from Wednesday. Perhaps
there's one who looks like my socialist father. How he marched and
drank Johnny Walker 'til he died. Perhaps there's more than a few
who resemble my older brother.

9.
How he stood Airforce and affirmatively proud with his hands in his
pockets seconds before his nerves broke. How he stood Airforce and
affirmatively proud every day after. I imagine in the millions the
sons and grandsons I may still have. The husband. The lover. All my
men. All my scars.

10.
The doctor folds his arms across his chest, gives me a suspicious bill
of good health. Jack is going, but not gone. I have a follow up date in
the not so distant future.

11.
Future. I march to an infusion room. In the infusion room is cable
television: C-Span, CNN, BET. In the infusion room the chemomonster
commands. Today it's sleeping. The I.V. pole glares in a corner. I
cover it with my coat, close the infusion room door, push the power
button on the television set, raise the volume, raise a fist, sit very
close, bow my head.

12.
During six months of chemotherapy I may have seen four black
patients. This number may be one too many. But the four or five of
us exchanged eyes. Whenever words were given, we spoke of family
members, professions, ages of children, a school's location—just in
case.

13.
I asked my chemo nurse where do most of the black cancer patients
of Central New York receive treatments. She nearly whispered, "they
die, it's a growing national concern." She's the only black chemo
nurse in this clinic.

14.
She's the only.

15.
Despite method or message the Great Lawn in front of the White
House in Washington D.C. America, October 16th isn't big enough. The
black men go way back, on fences as if to lift them, not ride them, in
trees as if growing, not being lynched, walking the waters of the
nation's reflecting pools. Going way back. How many named Malcolm,
how many named Martin, how many named Medgar, how many
named Moses? Way back.

16.
October 16th 1995 in my infusion room no burning veins, no raw
stomach. No Jack. Encouraged and inspired I want to take over this
room, march on the ceiling, rally my breath and breast against the
walls and floor, make banners of my arms and legs which read "free
me!" "free all of me now!" Afterwards, after every piece of me goes
home, washes, eats, I want to climb into the monster's bed, fall down
between someone's thighs, come into this haunted room with
something other than fear. This is victory. This is desire. This is blue.
This is October 16th 1995.

17.
I lock the infusion room door, secure my coat on the I.V. pole, look
around the room; a near empty box of tissues, a red pail for toxic
tears. I look at the televised and prime time black men hold hands
and sway. I sit closer to those hands. I sway. Look around the room
again; the hard candies in a small glass jar, the perfect shine of the
chrome faucet, the unexpected heat. I unbutton my blouse. What am
I asking to take place here, what am I daring this room to become?

18.
I have a dream. Prayers and speeches surround me.

19.
Privately, without shame or fear, under the soft wool of my dress I
touch the television screen, outline a few of the million, smile at
some, call to some, moan.

20.
Deep blue. Deep, deep blue.

21.
A prayer ends. I button my blouse. Open the door. My chemo nurse opens a window. The monster's courtyard is filled with heartbeat and breathing.

gale jackson

gale jackson, born in 1958, is a writer, a storyteller, and a librarian at Medgar Evers College, City University of New York. Her work has appeared in many journals, including IKON, Callaloo, Ploughshares, *and* Kenyon Review. *Her publications include a collaborative anthology with poets Kimiko Hahn and Susan Sherman.*

Fugitive Slaves . . .

I.

1711.

Paramarimbo
she sees nothing but mountains
nothing but mountains mounting
plains
by foot
by hand
by mouth
by god
by everything
she's got
she sees nothing but mountains
eyes full of sky and blood
and blood
she won't tell them
where the runaways hide
so they cut off her head

ogun
ogun
ogun

Paramarimbo
name her flora
she run
name her Sery
fat for the market
she run

she run
she run
wild mountains forest orchid
in this place
called Surinam
the Dutch make slaves
of Africans
and hunt them
when she ran first
they cut her achilles tendon
still
feet like flippers
she ran again
beat her burn her can't be owned
in the flames
she sees nothing but mountains
nothing but mountains mounting
plains
by foot
by hand
by mouth
by god
by everything
she's got
she sees nothing but mountains
eyes full of sky and blood
and blood
and she won't tell them
where the runaways hide
so they cut off her head . . .

II.

1741.
Brazil.
"They came to me.
say they had visions.
say 'sister you a healer'
and you see how we is
torn lips
chained lips
irons for legs
purple skin gone sage

gone sick
words brand
in our back
nigga
whore
slave
bitch
They came to me
to me
and I was a cup soaked full
and the words became hills
nine horses and the wind
a knife
for each one
it's death sure if they catch us
but we willing to kill
or be killed."

III.

1772.
Leogane

Ogun
Ogun
Ogun
she sings to me
iron bearer
girl with the red dress
she sing she scream
they run
they run
they run
Ogun
Ogun
Ogun
Leogane
Zabeth is my name
I live
in chains
Zabeth is my name
dog
in the yard

I live in chains
I eat chains
I eat chains
iron
fingers
blood
Zabeth is not my name
when I escape from them
the dogs chase me
Leogane
but
they can only kill me
once
Ogun
Ogun
Ogun
I
am the hunted
hunting
a woman
actually
a girl
ghost legs
iron bearer
red dress
wearer
where
oh where
Ogun
Ogun
Ogun
Ogun

IV.

1850
North America.

Jacintha, Clarissa Davis, Maria Dorsey, Jane Johnson
Louisa Brown, Charity Still, Arrah Weams, Chloe
Ellen Craft alias some white man
Emeline Chapman alias Susan Bell

Maria Weams alias Joe Wright
alias Ellen Capron alias
Rose Ann McDonald
Charlotte Green
Leer Green
Harriet Elgin
General
Harriet Tubman
Harriet Ann Jacobs
alias
Linda
Brent
jumped
from
masters bedroom window
crawled low changed hands changed names
crossed her heart to die for those she left behind
hid in an attic for seven years

Ogun

bore fifteen children
saw brute work kill ten went
mute with the pain and ran across
the state of Maryland before she spoke again

Ogun

one child holding each of her fingers
bigger ones trusting the sureness of her hem
Jane Johnson took six of them across the state lines
to Philadelphia freedom

Ogun

Leer Green
what you wouldn't do for love
packed herself into a trunk and mailed it
Lu
costumed by her skin and a freshed pressed man's shirt
walked on to a boat like she was coming to work and just sailed out
Juba danced

Juba danced
whirling like a flock of doves into the Alantic ocean
before the slavers realized the waves was swallowing their wares

Ogun
Ogun
Ogun
ooooooooooooooooooooooooooooooooo.

V.

Barbados South Carolina

dressed as night
dressed as men
naked below every stitch
they owned
with children
though they could hold you down
with other women with men
alone
with love with strangers
with darkness covering
bread in their pockets seeds
in their hair bare foot
bare hands
bare headed
in the wind
taking off with a song
making love and then
words beckoned them
steal away if you can
if not slap shit outta somebody
and run
piedra
aurora
witch hairs of corn
dogs howl stars wild
some women ran
at twilight
some women ran
at dawn

before the day begin
again.

VI.

We was in the fields
called them "Carolinas"
called us planting rice
under lash
we call back and forth
from the time the moon lay on her back
till she stood up to see the night
through the sun's whole walk
"now?" i call out to the oldest one
but she call back
"not yet"
lash
catch my back and the sun keep rising
till i sing out
"when?"
though she sing back
"wait"
sun hot hot
taste a leather in my mouth
i sing soft
"oh lord, oh lord, oh lord"
till she sing
"yes"
and by God we a burst
hoe drop
line break
we run
we run
we run
six of us
not minding the lash
or the cock of a gun
we run
faster
and faster
and faster
till we the wind

we the wind
and we takes
the wind takes
and we bears us up
and we gives us wings. . . . . . .
Ogun
Ogun
Ogun[1]

Alice

1686–1802
Toll taker at Dunk's Ferry, Pennsylvania.

Guiding this ferry across the river
sometimes I pause
in the water's center
to cast a thought with my line out
for fish.

Lived so long city grown from forest
around me and my memory serves
as history in this county
where they call on a slave boatswoman
to hear the story before theirs
of wigwams longhouse wolves and panthers
howling the river fat with trout
the sky black with birds flying
God's gardening.

1. Most written sources and much oral lore tells us that African and African American women escaped from slavery much less often than did men. Children, family, community commitments as well as the women's sense of identity as inextricable from them all contributed to their tendency to avoid the life of the fugitive slave. Still many women did run, and this poem is a recollection of them. The names and stories of North American women after 1800 are from William Still's *The Underground Railroad* (1872), where Still compiled the interviews he conducted with the men and women who passed through the Philadelphia station that he, a fugitive slave himself, helped to operate. The stories of Caribbean women before 1800 are from Eduardo Galeano's *Memory of Fire* (1987). The idea of "slapping the shit out of someone" to escape is taken from Silvia DuBois's tough memoir, and perhaps it is her verve that reminded me of the continuities of the African gods even in North America. Ogun, the Yoruba god of hunters and metal and accidents and war, became a banner for resistance through most of the African diaspora and though this cultural presence is most evident in the maroon societies of the Caribbean I imagine it "mounting" the heads of Africa's North American children as well.

Can't no one sail faster or surer
than this here black woman set loose
against the wind taut line there
in my hand feet steadying the skiff
and sometimes I stop in the water
to toss out a line and consider
freedom.[2]

Some of
Betty's Story
round 1850

Snowed.
They took
two good stepping horses
but we didn't ride
Mama Emma Mae me and a few others
were fastened to them by chains on our ankles
and our hands
walking to Texas barefoot but chained Master
running west from trouble back in Georgia.
Before we left he branded my mother burned
his signature between her breast and they was
still pus and sore but the raw hide whip
keep the weak moving just the same.
Her name was Betty.
After some days walking
her feet got to bleeding ice eat the flesh
she fall
horse chain tear off her little bit of clothes
she moans
we all moans

2. Alice was known as an oral historian and storyteller in colonial Philadelphia though, like many of her African woman compatriots, only a glimpse of her own life story survives her. According to the 1804 publication *Eccentric Biography; or Memoirs of Remarkable Female Characters Ancient and Modern* (Philadelphia), Alice was born into life and slavery in 1686 to parents who had been sold from Barbados to New England. (Few writers in general and fewer historians in particular have looked carefully at the "link" cross-fertilizing the African diaspora populations that, in the early years of the Atlantic slave trade, came first through the West Indies into the slave societies of North America. Important keys to understanding African American migrations of identity are buried there.) Alice's household moved from Philadelphia to Dunks Ferry, Pennsylvania, when she was ten and she spent the rest of her life working there as a toll taker at the ferry, a fisherwoman, and a boatswoman.

then she choose to die straining against
the horse her open breast
Mama falls and hugs the ground
though Master cuss and draw his gun
he can't shoot her further down one two three four
times then he raise the whip force the weak to walk
coffle move on leaving her behind to be buried
as the snow falls coffle moves on
but she stays with us in mind.[3]

3. To say simply that between such and such a date enslaved Africans and African Americans were forcibly moved in a significant "migration" out of the upper south and into the lower south and the west seems to be an abomination of the supposed victors' rendering. The narratives of Sally, Betty, and many of the other men and women who were torn from their families again and again to feed the hungry mouth of this nation's economy tell both an old and a continuing story. I was moved by the recollection of Ted Simpson in the WPA narrative collection to rewrite his mother's story. Even though I cannot hear her voice, her moan and then her silence haunts me.

Major L. Jackson

Major L. Jackson, born in 1968, is a graduate of Temple University and is the poetry curator of the Painted Bride Art Center in Philadelphia. A member of the Dark Room Collective, he has held artist residencies at the MacDowell Colony and at the Third Avenue Performance Space in Columbus, Ohio. He is coediting an anthology, Sixty Million & More: Writings on the Middle Passage.

Blunts

The first time I got high I stood in a circle
of boys at 23rd & Ridge tucked inside
a doorway that smelled of piss. It was
March, the cold rains all but blurred
our sight as we feigned sophistication and
rapped about the honeyed-dew ebb
of youth. Johnny Cash, who would tap
his brother's stash, had a love
for transcendental numbers and felt—
in between puffs resembling little gasps
of air—the link to all creation was
the mathematician. Malik, the smartest
of the crew, counter-argued and cited the holy
life of prayer and sacrifice as a gateway
into the Islamic faith, that was for all intents,
the true path for the righteous black man.
No one disputed. Malik cocked his head,
pinched the joint and pulled so hard we imagined
his lips crazy-glued into stiff "O"s. It was long
agreed that Lefty would inherit his father's
used car business; thus destined for a life of wrecks.
Then, in between a fit of coughing, I broke
the silence. "I want to be a poet." I remember
it was nearing dinner-time. Jesus lived here.
His sister was now yelling at their younger siblings
over the faint sounds of evening news and game shows.
The stench of hot dogs and sauerkraut drifted
down the dank hallway. A pre-spring wind flapped
the plastic covering of a junkman's shopping cart
as Eddie Hardrick licked from left to right the thin

strip of glue bordering the edge of a rolling
paper, then uttered, "So, you want the tongue
of God." At that moment I doubled over
in the haze of smoke and looked up for help.
It was too late; we were tragically hip.

Some Kind of Crazy

It doesn't matter if you can't see
Steve's 1985 Corvette: Turquoise-colored,
Plush purple seats, gold-trimmed
Rims that make little stars in your eyes

As if the sun is kneeling, kissing
The edge of sanity. Like a Baptist
Preacher stroking the dark underside
Of God's wet tongue, he can make you

Believe. It's there, his scuffed wing-
Tips—ragged as a mop, shuffling
Concrete—could be ten-inch Firestone
Wheels, his vocal chords fake

An eight cylinder engine that wags
Like a dog's tail as he shifts gears. Imagine
Steve, moonstruck, cool, turning right
Onto Ridge Avenue, arms forming

Arcs, his hands a set of stiff C's
Overthrowing each other's rule,
His lithe body and head snap back
Pushing a stick shift into fourth

Whizzing past Uncle Sam's Pawn
Shop, past Chung Phat's Stop & Go.
Only he knows his destination,
His limits. Can you see him? Imagine

Steve, moonstruck, cool, parallel,
Parking between a Pacer and a Pinto—
Obviously the most hip—backing up,
Head over right shoulder, one hand

Spinning, polishing a dream;
And there's Tina, wanting to know
What makes a man tick, asks him
For a ride. For a moment, he comes

Back, returns, wonders if he can
Fulfill the promise. Not a second
Further she bends, slides in
Pretending never to be seen again.

We, the faithful, never call
Him crazy, crackbrained, just a little
Touched. It's all he ever wants, a car,
A girl, a community of believers.

Don Pullen at the Zanzibar
Blue Jazz Cafe, 1994

Half-past eight Don Pullen just arrived
from Yellow Springs. By his side
is the African-Brazilian Connection.
If it were any later, another space,
say "Up All Night Movie Hour"
on Channel 7, he might have been
a cartel leader snorting little mountains
of cocaine up his mutilated nostrils
from behind his bureau as he buries
a flurry of silver-headed bullets
into the chests of the good guys;
an armlock M-16 in his right hand,
a sawed-off double barrel shotgun
in his left, his dead blond
girlfriend oozing globules of blood
by the jacuzzi. Nothing, no one,
could be cooler balancing all
those stimulants. No one. She said

she couldn't trust me, that her
ladybugs were mysteriously
disappearing, that I no longer
sprinkle rose petals in her
bath, that some woman left a bouquet

of scented lingerie and a burning
candelabra on our doorstep, that she
was leaving, off to France, Paris—
the land of real lovers. In this club,
the dim track lights reflecting off
the mirror where the bottles are lined
like a firing-line studying their targets
makes the ice, stacked on top of ice,
very sexy, surprisingly beautiful and this
is my burden; I see Beauty in everything,
everywhere. How can one cringe upon
hearing of a six year old boy, snatched
from a mall outside of London, two
beggarly boys luring him to the train
tracks with a bag of popcorn only to beat
his head into a pulp of bad cabbage!
Smell them, holding his hand promising
Candyland in all its stripes and chutes.
What chaste and immaculate evil!

Nine-fifteen, Don and the African-
Brazilian have lit into *Capoiera*.
The berimbau string stings my eyes
already blurring cognac, my eyes
trying to half-see if that's my muse
sitting up front, unrecognizable,
a specter. Don's wire fingers are
scraping up the ivory keys, off-
rhythm. It doesn't matter, the Connection
agrees there's room as they sway
and fall against the ceiling, a band
of white shadows wind-whipped
on a clothesline. Don's raspy hands,
more violent than a fusillade of autumn
leaves falling like paper rain in blazing
reds and yellows along East River Drive
bangs, hammers away, shivers in
monstrous anarchy. Don's arms arch

like orange slices squirting on my mouth's
roof, juice everywhere. His body swings
upward and we are left less ambitious.
The audience, surveying each other's

emotions, feel the extensions; their bodies
meld into the walls, leaving a funeral
of fingerprints as they exhale back
to their seats. Ten minutes to twelve, I'm
waving a taxi like a madman. I will tell her
about tonight, tell her how a guy named Don
and his crew, The Connection destroyed scales,
hacked harmonies, banged piano keys
into a mush of fudge ice cream, all in rhythm,
all in sweet harsh contradictions.

Harriet Jacobs

Harriet Jacobs was born in 1951 and lives and works in Los Angeles. Her work has been anthologized in In Search of Color Everywhere: An Anthology of African-American Poetry *and* Nommo II: Remembering Ourselves Whole. *Her poetry appears frequently in* Catalyst *magazine.*

goree

if i stretch my neck all the way
to the left, it's there reduced by
distance
to the size of my palm
but as blue as i remembered it.
then i can breathe. sometimes
i hear laughter, but it sounds far away.
i know it doesn't come from the darkness.
the woman on my left moans all the time now
and does not sit up. if she dies
maybe i will get her spot.
at night i try to remember the pieces of blue
and keep breathing
all night long
i pray to the ancestors in my head
asking them to let me breathe
all day i wonder
what kind of people are these
who would give you only a piece
of the sky?

and sometimes i hear this song in my head

we have always heard music
found ways to smooth back the edges
of madness
stretched our voices
to the slap of oar against water
heard blues in the snap of cotton breaking
from stem
we always been a music

people
sometimes lost in a jungle of tears
but we keep finding our way back
to that
clearing
at the center
of our selves
where the trees still talk to us
and our tongues keep remembering the rhythm
of the words we forgot
swaying on the backs of buses
and in hot kitchens
crooning
in pool halls and shared bathrooms
yeah/we carving a heartspace
and staring down the darkness some call our future
and they saying it be just dope and more dope
and no hope
and they don't even see we all the time
standing in the middle of the trees
and steady singing
you can't
you can't
you can't
touch this

imagination in flight: an improvisational duet

we could say
it was a saxophone flight
thru some new music/ we ridin sonic riffs
over to cantaloupe island
or some other sticky-fingered
fulla juice place   /toe painting graffiti
on the roof of the sky   maybe we could say
we dissolving old vendettas
& stakin out new turf
like crip & blood sliding into
an easy truce/   you/warm
& melting like chocolate down the back of my throat
could be a long deep swallow of hours
making stars fall down thru this night

like a shower of topnotes/   we might even
get caught up inside some unnamed place
most people never even get to
& not be seen again/ ya know
maybe we oughta leave a note
hinting at the whereabouts of such possibilities
as how you filling up all my empty spaces
with warm sounds/   like
a hornplayer do
tenderly tonguing his reed
into a pliant state of readiness   /could be us
dancing a slow samba to the rhythm
of remembering/   or even the way the smell of the country
likes to lay itself out/   nuzzling up close
to freshly turned damp earth holding on
ya know lingering softly/ like mist
after a spring rain   oh yes   i think maybe
we could call it/   something
like that

growing into my name
for harriet tubman

worn like a hand-me-down
unfashionable   unasked for
a quiet stitching of syllables
apart   from the boisterous crowd
of cheryls jackies and debbies
you oldwoman ghost ridin hard
on my young girl shoulders
wasn't no soft name i was given/ no
something about the cadence
or maybe it was the weight of history marching across the tongue
that held me captive
disallowing total escape
into the mindlessness of youth
until somewhere in me
i remembered
now i pray
and stretch my heart and limbs
to fit this cloak painted with the nameless faces
of stars

the sound of your name steady as my own breath
your iron will knitting my spine
i hear the rush of secrets
in your eyes and
now
i cannot look at the sky
without seeing your name spelled out
in the passing of clouds
over the moon
danger has a familiar smell about it
and on moonless nights
i put candles in my hair

                                        and wait

by the side of the road

on extending the olive branch
to my own self

what was i doing anyway
was i crazy did i think
that by beating it into submission
i would win something
i've witnessed other casualties of war
the eyes of madness
that wandered through my neighborhood
after nam   what made me think
self-inflicted war would be
more merciful
or that oils & lubricants
metal combs of fire/chemical assault/all the
forces that modern technology could marshal
would ever win out over mother nature
& tell me this/ what made me think
that would be a victory
anyway

a postscript
to my brothers and sisters:

it matters not how we wear it
but if we begin to wrap ourselves
just as tightly around each other

& refuse to let go
if we rise up mighty like a dark cloud
& resist all efforts to change the nature
of who we really are
when we learn to stand
just as unshakable
in the beauty of our strength
and the strength of our beauty
then

then . . .

about our hips

our hips,
they a poem to pulchritude
they sing anthems to negritude,
our hips   they smooth and sweet
as candied yams, and fine as grandma's
home cured ham
they beauty—it was not designed
to be resrained by calvin klein
they smile and giggle, they laugh out loud
they free and full, they strong and proud
our hips hold secrets from the past,
and hold our future in their grasp
our hips got motions known to tease
made james brown sing
some please please please
our hips,
make brothers thank the lord above
they got sweet hips like ours
to love

Valerie Jean

Valerie Jean, born in 1953, graduated from the University of Maryland with an MFA in poetry in 1989. She has published in Missouri Review, The River Styx, Black American Literature Forum, *and* Callaloo. *She was winner of the 1991 Artscape Literary Arts Award in Baltimore, an event that resulted in the publication of her chapbook,* Woman Writing a Letter.

Lesson on Braces

I was twelve, and did not
want braces, horrified
at the prospect of steel
stuffed between my teeth.
Throwing brash tantrums,
I begged not to have wire
crammed into my mouth.

I woke up nights drenched,
with the sounds of marching,
imagined boot prints left
stomped into my tongue.
I heard the metal scrape,
worse than chalk on the
board, become the object

of cruel schoolyard taunts.
I dreamed of locked cages
where my voice imploded,
but that night I saw blood
gush from my lips, then pool
in a rising ocean that was
threatening to drown me,

my roaring reverberated
past the dawn, where morning
found me beached between
my parents' anxious concern.
That day, I insisted that

I knew what I did not want,
knew what was unnecessary,

what would hurt me. I was
young enough to be dismissed,
and dragged off, screaming,
to the dentist chair anyway.
Yet, my ragged-tooth smile
remains, a testament to my
father's extraordinary,

yet simple acknowledgement—
"*Well, it is her mouth and
if she doesn't want braces . . .*"—
that I have the right to
speak all that I know and
feel, and that I only have
to endure unavoidable pain.

On Apologies

You were half-right, I did lie,
telling Miss Cooley you had hurt me.
I didn't feel that punch, you just
caught me off-balance. I got scared,
had to make her believe I hadn't
hurt you on purpose. We both knew
I did. I'd heard what you said to
John, talking loud, meaning for me

to catch your meaning, a crude blow,
from across the full schoolyard. I
pretended it was dirt stuck in my eye.
No one else seemed to notice. I almost
forgot after recess, me and Mary Beth
giggling about some silliness. Being
nine, we were prone to such fits. But
you were also nine, and also half-wrong.

Do you remember how you pushed me,
acting like you had a right to, acting

like I had no right to a drink of water?
You knocked me down, shoved me right
out of your way. Remember how my skirt
blew up, how my underwear spread laughter
throughout the room? Even Mary Beth,
my best white friend, was laughing.

That made me crazy. Then, remembering
what you had said, I wanted to hurt you.
Miss Cooley had stepped out, leaving
us to handle this one on our own. We
blew it. As I jumped up at you, both
your fists hung, cocky. You did not
know I was used to fighting from my guts.
Raging mad, I wanted to kill you. You

barely grazed my stomach with that sorry
swing, when I drew back and kicked the hell
out of your leg. Your face went blank,
your eyes reeled, wild. For a second,
I felt quite sick at your horror. You
could not help the way your body went
limp, falling over desks in slow motion.
In the silence of the room, the steps

of Miss Cooley echoed from the hall.
I froze, knowing I was in deep trouble.
I knew I had kicked you harder than I
should have. You could barely move,
the wind still gone from your shocked
lungs. You managed to get up in time
for Miss Cooley to see you lunge at me,
to hear you cursing. I started to cry,

as she wedged between us, a large oak.
Terrified, I watched you yell, trying
to get to me, acting out your pain
or, perhaps, you mistook my tears for
weakness. You carried on so bad that
Miss Cooley dragged you to the office.
I knew I was going to get it, going
to get whipped real good, and twice

too, since Mr. Keyes had warned me
about my temper and mamma had said
I'd better not be in the middle of
no more fighting at school. I knew
Mr. Keyes would see the bruise I had
marked you with and would pull his
paddle off the wall, bend me over
his desk, again, make me holler. So

when she bent down, Miss Cooley, to hug
me, I couldn't help exaggerating how
you punched me in my stomach, how much
it still hurt. I couldn't stop crying,
which surprised me, since it wasn't like
me to be so upset in public. I think
that was the reason Mr. Keyes believed
me when he did ask what had started

the whole thing. I never told him
about your words. I had to make him
believe my story, which came much more
fleshed out in the second telling,
going over how you had pushed me to
the ground, admitting I had kicked you,
but only after you had punched me in
the stomach really hard! Miss Cooley

got behind me then, straightening even
Mr. Keyes in his place. Pointing her
quick finger in your face, she was
shouting in that high-pitched tone that
meant she was dead serious. But she
was screaming at *you*, telling *you* that
you *never hit a girl*, "Mister, not in my
classroom, especially not in her stomach!

Girls have too many delicate parts down
there!" Mr. Keyes took over, calling you
out in front of everybody for punching me,
a girl, in my stomach. I nearly forgot
my predicament as I watched you follow
him, trying not to limp, trying to pretend

I hadn't hurt you at all. Mary Beth's
sly wink and that worried look of hers

reminded me to keep up my act. I got
the rest of the afternoon off, recovering
in the sick room. When I came back,
the next day, your eyes rolled past me.
We never spoke again, all through junior
high and high school, although we saw
each other often. I always felt there
was unfinished business between us.

I wonder what you told your parents,
if they had beat you, like my mamma
would have done me, or what they must
have said about me, seeing that blue
mark scarring your leg. Did they believe
you, telling the truth of how I rocked
you, or did you never tell them, afraid
to admit being beat up by a "nigger" girl?

I wondered if I ought to apologize, what
you would say if I ever tried. I never
did, but I had nightmares and broken sleep.
Being Catholic, I assumed God was punishing
me for lying, so I suffered until I got
the courage to confess my sin at church.
But I never went back to see Miss Cooley
like Father Michaels said I should. In

my heart, I could never take it back,
figuring I would just have to burn in hell.
I often wondered about my delicate parts,
if Mr. Keyes convinced you? Would you
remember why we fought, and if so, being
older now, like me, could you admit that
it was your words, not your fists that hurt
me? Could you tell me you were sorry, too?

A. Van Jordan

A. Van Jordan was born in 1965 and raised in Akron, Ohio. He is a graduate of Wittenburg University and Howard University. He works with the WritersCorps program in Washington, D. C., and has participated in the Ascension Poetry Reading Series directed by E. Ethelbert Miller.

If I Write a Poem . . .

and then I smile and title it
"Black is Beautiful,"
and lift it to my lips
like a brass horn
and blow life's musics,
will you think I'm angry?
Or should I retreat from this battle
and go back to my innocence?

A time when my best friend was white,
and I came home asking
why is he better than me
because I'm something called a "Nigger"?
"It's not true," my father said,
"He shouldn't have used such a bad word."
His caveat: Stay away from him until
his parents teach him better.

Will I ever learn from the experience
as a fifth grader, my brother and I
walking through a shopping plaza—
in Cuyahoga Falls, Ohio,
enjoying a taste of the "other shade
of green," when squad cars pulled up,
cops pulled out guns,
grabbed, and frisked over our dream?
My mother, full of life's
history lessons, asked, "Why?"
And the shop owners, who smiled politely;
and the police, who were just doing their jobs;
and the witnesses, being good citizens, shrugged,
"Because ma'am, they looked suspicious."

And then if I wear wax wings
of black pride flying
out of range of verses
like, "You know, college is not for everyone—"
verses my high school counselor used
on me—will you be too young
and kind to understand
the gravity of my voice?

Do I fly
too close to the sun
if I write lines that show
me not quite getting it,
not wanting to hear,
on a night filled with
friends and stardust walks
the disturbing hiss of kegged beer
spraying over our bodies
and the hissing words of this car's occupants,
driving by, reminding me, I never learned
the meaning of that "N" word.

But, you see, if I write a poem now
measuring line and meter,
listening to sounds of my own life,
holding my loss of innocence over
and over again, I can find—
in these discordant moments—music.

A Dance Lesson

When you discovered
    I had been taking
dance lessons
    with the daughters
of your union
    brothers from the plant,
you raised hell.
    You looked at my mother.
Told her:
    "you're goin' to turn him

into a fag."
    My chicanery had fooled
her and my dance instructor.
    And now, she had to pay
for my little ruse.
    She thought I was taken
with dance,
       while really
I chased and two-stepped
    my way into the hearts
of young girls.
    I got the lead
in Peter Pan
    and I became
Mr. Bojangles,
    all to chase girls.
She would have been
    so disappointed
to see me act
    so like you, but,
if you had known,
    you would have been so proud.

My Father's Retirement

It's been 50 years since
he lied about his age,
strutted through the doors
of the Goodyear plant,
and asked for work
like he would ask a woman to dance:
with respect for her,
with confidence in himself.

He's wielded his service
like any chosen weapon
of the industrial worker:
the benefits, holiday pay,
and company picnics
protected his family.
He cherished that job more

than marriage; held it longer
than he'd held any woman.

And why not?
At 14—when his father left—
there was a light turned off in his life.
He seized the torch,
lit the path,
served a generation
of siblings
and children
and mamas.
And now, leads me
on my dark workday mornings.
When I drag from bed,
I see him.
He's a lighthouse,
through my daily labors,
guiding me in.

Shirley Bradley LeFlore

Shirley Bradley LeFlore, born in 1940, is a poet, performance artist, and psychologist. She is currently associate professor of African American literature at the University of Missouri, St. Louis. Her work has appeared in Black American Literature Forum *and in anthologies such as* A Turn in the River: Anthology in Celebration of Gwendolyn Brooks *and* Aloud: Voices from the Nuyorican Poets Cafe.

Dream/Eaters

Dream/eaters on the edge
Broken like glass on the edge

They wear no mask/just the wind
Bloodrunners w/fire between their ears/on the edge
They swallow the sun/chew on the moon
Star-studded teeth light up the air/on the edge
They are the war
Unlisted soldier/our battlescars/on the edge

Dream/eaters/on the edge

They celebrate their own "Rights of Passage"
Avenging their ancestors/revenge of the middle-passage/
On the edge/they confuse the unjust/w/just-us
Dreameater/just -ice/on the edge
They smoke dreams/choke dreams/stomp dreams/on the edge
You can smell them before daybreak
You can see their shadows at high-noon/on the edge
Dream/eaters/on the edge

Dream/eaters suck eyes, sweet-eyes/innocent eye/
Free and easy eyes/stone eyes/bitter eyes/old eyes/
Bold eyes/doo doo eyes/bitch eyes
They suck eyes w/angry straws/on the edge

Eye-sucking dream/eaters/on the edge
Dying w/wet soggy dreams/on the edge
In the streets/on the edge/in the arms of a hot funky-beat
On the edge/they just die and die and die/on the edge

With no cooling board/no winding sheet/no metal/no honor
Backs against their tomorrows unborn
They die and die and die/die/die/ on the edge

With just one crystal tear
Trapped in the fear of a mother's scream . . . . STOP!

Rayboy Blk & Bluz
For Arthur R. Brown

I rememba
Rayboy blu/blk bug-eyed wid yo chocolate smile
When you wuz jes knee-hi   to a hoppergrass
And time was 1/2 pass a monkey's ass
Memba—when you wuz jes a lil scuttle-butt/jr. flip
Hip-dipped in the mouth of the south
Tongue pluckin cotton in the mississippi bottoms

Memba—you sittin roun' yo grandaddies ankles
Eye suckin his footprints—soppin yo history like a
Biscuit doin gravy—collectin yo shadows—sharpenin yo
Wings on the teeth of yo ancesters—tucking them words
In yo hip-pocket w/yo chocolate smile and yo lil boogie-bugle
You wuz passin-off for a trumpet

I memba
Rayboy blu/blk and bug-eyed
When them white sheets lit up the night like toe-jam fever
When yo daddie did a twofisted nigga-knuckle dance on a
Crackers ass and less then 3 days he was pushin up daisies
Underneath tha ole Magnolia tree and the low-dixie wind wuz
Whistling a breeze around that ole rugged burnt out cross
And yo momma's tears wuz proud mary

I memba
You playin on yo 2 string guitar in the out-house
When you swore on a capone and a rooster that some day you
Wuz gona take Gabriel to a duel befo that great gittin-up
Morning said you wuz gon take him down solo so low said you
Wuz gona smack him w/a vamp and then snatch one of yo
Poems outcha lil-hip   pocket and word-whoop him to death wid
Yo good-foot strong as red-devil lye and dare him to rise

I rememba—memba
When you said you wuz gon-gitup- git-up and bird do a
Lite foot and hummin shuffle, git on that Rock Island Line
That side-winds at the junction roun-midnite/said you wuz gon
Put some dust between you and them death-hounds breath'n on
Yo heels/said you wannit to blow—you an yo 2-bit boogie-bugle
You wuz passin-off for a trumpet/said you wannit to blow-blast
Some real brass/do a shu-shu/bop-hop wid yo hip lip an/a rebop
Vamp/do a rap so boss that it tie-up a chinese tongue an make
bricks outa wigwom and a hut
Said you wuz goin to St. Louis an take that long-legged/SWAMP-
WATER WOMAN wid you—cuz that 2-headed snapper between her
Thighs you jus did'nt wanna leave behind

I rememba/memba/mema/ yeh
Rayboy blu/blk bug-eyed wid yo chocolate smile
And that 2-bit boogie bugle—yeh you traded it for a
Trumpet an every mawning I can hear you blow

This Poem

This is a spirit poem
Beating my breast like a drum
Talking up a storm
Coming hooploop and crazyhorse
Painting Red-Cloud and Black Elk
Singing Geronimo

Speaking the great-tongue of
Earthmother Rainbow
Listening to skywalkers pray
For Leonard Peltier
Wounded in the knee and heart
With the waterbuffalo   spreadeagle

This is a spirit poem

When the mountain carried a windsong
in its bosom
And the valley cradled the footprints of God
And bird/beast/field/flower/man and sky were family

This is a spirit poem
Before the terrorist came

Humpedback and foothoofed
Riding the ironhorse
The taste of power in their lefthand
Foaming at the mouth and a killing/eye

A spirit poem/a poem w/a memory
Doing a flashback

Beating the hell out of truth
With a sack full of
Tricks and treatise
Signed in blood and lies
And peace broken like glass

A spirit poem/a poem w/a memory
Doing a flashback

Singing squawstealing and bloodmixing
With nature moaning menred
Dead feathers in their head
On reservations and rations

This is a spirit poem
Before the terrorist came

This is a spirit poem
Beating my breast like a drum
Hot like juju

a sweatin/soulin poem

Dragging swansongs and silence like night
And rusted chains w/no grace
Pulling the weepin and wailin
Like billows rolling and breakers dashing
Thru muddywaters bloody
Once gold like yams

a sweatin/soulin poem

With screaming in the eye
Rocking and rolling time
Of renegades and runaways
And the Arkansaw brownskin soldiers
Copper/eyes and licorice feet
Purple faces/nutmeg hands
In a desperate land
Sheetwrapped Klans
Knees scarred and circles broken

A sweatin/soulin poem
A hangin poem/ a raping poem
A court and elder poem
A charging poem

Charging terrorist and thieves
With stolen property/stolen birthrights
And people and dreams and visions
Choking saints w/jesus in a gunnysack

This is a spirit poem w/a memory
Doing a flashback

Talking about shingles and shit/true/grit
And grime and dirty hearts and hands
And pimps playing GOD and NASTY
On the smoothgreen of capitol hill
While peasants pay the bill

This is a spirit poem SCREAMINNNNNN

WAR   /   WHAT FOR ?????????
Hiroshima/   Vietnam/   Grenada/El Salvador
Nicaragua/   Panama/South-Africa/Mississippi
Alabama/Chicago/   A/MERRI/CAN

A screamin poem
For the hungry/the homeless/diseased/dis-eased
Violence/violins and Ola Mae's babies

A screamin poem
Heaving in my bosom
Knocking on my tombstone

Hailing Mary/weeping and wailing
Yelling and screaming
A breakdown and rappin poem

SCREAMINNNN

This is a Spirit poem
A today poem
Doing a drumcall/drumtalking in word
In rhythm and sometimes rhyme
Calling men/women/children
With short/eyes/wrist/ankle/lips/and/hearts
Wringing like ole rags

This is a today poem/a callin poem
And somebodys got to be blessed

A woman calling poem to walk in grace
Thru her storm, suck up the light drink
Fresh water take her place in the sun
And be healed

A man calling poem to rise up make his bed gather
His courage his strength his tender his loins
his babies his women
And be healed

A children calling poem to smother the anger of their
Nowness soak-up the sunshine of their newness feel the power
Of their dreams their vision see all the good inside and be
Sing a lovesong for their tomorrow unborned
And be healed

Calling the prophet/the preacher/the priest/politician
Physician to be healed

This is a today poem/a callin poem/a healing poem
And somebodys got to be blessed

> **This is not a revelation poem**
> **But a revolution poem**
> **Because revolutions are borned**

Out of the evolution of every
Generation

This poem may never be heard
But it will keep on hearing
This poem may never be seen
But it will keep on seeing

SO DON'T TRY TO KILL THIS POEM
JUST KEEP WRITING
                    THIS POEM . . . .

Norman Loftis

Norman Loftis was born in Chicago in 1943. He is a poet, novelist, essayist, and award-winning filmmaker. His credits include the poetry volume Black Anima *and the feature-length films* Small Time *and* The Messenger. *He is currently on the faculty of Medgar Evers College, City University of New York.*

Delirium

Now for my story. For many years
I was the glory of Chicago's southside.
I lived the life of the hip,
Thrilling to Coltrane's saxophone
And spoke a coded language
Only the initiate could understand.
Then I received my calling.
I moved to New York and remade
Myself completely. I went for long
Periods without eating red meat.
I frequently fasted on a diet of water
And sunflower seeds to make
My whole being an antenna for receiving
The most finely tuned poetic dictation.
I reserved all rights of rebroadcast.

I reinvented natural rhythms
Capable of stimulating common feeling tones
in any living species.
With expert ear, I conceived
A scale of gradiated sounds
That could visibly reproduce
All the colors of the rainbow.

In poetic visions, I saw the end
of all wars. I dreamed of a poetic
Language capable of discussing directly
With God without means of religion
Intermediacy what's gone wrong with man
And of discerning His plans for the future of mankind.

It was from the beginning
A desperate undertaking. I wrote
Poetry on the wind and thought in
Smoke signals. With lines
More powerful than lasers,
I stopped the flight of rocket ships.

Big John

His photograph, yellowed by the years,
shows him in a rural doorway,
grandmother glued to him
standing so reed straight
in the climate of his day
you think white men might have lynched him
for arrogance of posture.
His face with its broad, black features
has the ruggedness of men in westerns,
a resolutely decent human being
but capable of the most desperate acts
should Native Americans attack the wagontrain
or rich ranchers try to drive them from their land.

Maybe that's why the story
that he killed a man and had to flee Kentucky
doesn't surprise me,
why at even this distance
he can still inspire fear and awe.

How shall we praise this man?
Shall we say he was
A steam driller by trade,
his broad, black shoulders built Chicago subways,
jettisoned its trolley tracks,
paved its streets?

We can only calculate
in that time when lynchings
were still a part of the national landscape
what it cost him to hold a city job
and keep his temper

while everyone around him was losing theirs
and blaming it on him.

That's why Fridays
assume special significance.
He, like the others of his ilk
would gather in bars
and revenge themselves on each other.
It was a ritual as old
as human cruelty,
as universal as the rite
in which the women of our household,
like hyenas attacking a wounded lioness,
snapping and retreating from harm's way
separated granddaddy from his money
before he hit the streets.

Even in our section of Chicago's southside
that styled itself Dodge City
where a lawman called "Two Gun Pete,"
pearl handled forty fives on either thigh,
asked the congregating multitudes
to clear the street
and invariably had his way,
grandfather was a formidable figure
who stood no stuff and gave
no more than he could handle.

That he was capable of meanness,
even brutality is all too obvious.
He'd sometimes beat grandmother's
fat arms blue,
sending the whole household
into a screaming fury shouting threats of death.
But, when Sunday rolled around
with its breakfast of grits and buttermilk biscuits,
when Sunday rolled around
and he'd sit smoking his inevitable cigar
and reading the Sunday Sun Times,
he was once again the giver of gifts
and the heart as vast as an oceanliner
was open to request ranging from a cap gun to a car.

Some might have climbed Kilimanjaro.
Others aspired to the Senate
and praise themselves
with deserving accolades when they've succeeded,
but this man, son of a slave set free by Lincoln
as a boy, who as a man was angry-mean,
and Irish mother
he never mentioned til judgment day,
fighting the powers that be
and those within,
to become an average Joe
in an age that regarded him a zero to the nth degree,
this blackhole became a sun
around which smaller suns orbited
and were content.

Ruth

We caught fireflies,
punched holes in jars
and watched them
fly away with the night.

We squirreled up trees
and danced when we succeeded
on garage roofs,
or threw rocks,
two small children
with no suspicion
summer would end.

Pretty in pigtails,
your brown skin burnt amber,
your bony knees scraped
by activities indispensable
to the tomboy you were.
You were smart
and could pack a punch
that made me see stars.

When politicians wax poetic
about the way things used to be

only you and I are left
to remind them
how the milkman was mugged
in our alley
in broad daylight,
how the insurance man
in the inner lobby
suffered a similar fate.

And yet it's true,
despite immersion in the wordly
we had a shared innocence
that mistook a big box of condoms
for balloons and blew them up,
the moon for a wedding ring,
I slipped gently on your finger.

Fights After School

All the time the teacher
was going over the lesson
he was making faces at me
placing his squeezed fist on either eye
to indicate that would be my reward
when the school day was done.

My stomach churned. I wanted to disappear.
But when the bell rang to go
and anticipation of the day's main event mounted,
friends patting me on the back encouragingly,
I knew I had no choice.

Flung together by the crowd,
I lashed out with hatred and fear
at the boy who boxed my ear
and gave me a bloody nose besides.
Hitting him hard enough
to make him lose his balance and his will
to continue, I was on top of him
flailing with all my strength
on his bloody face,

afraid of what might happen
if suddenly he managed to wiggle free.

Brief Encounter

Before she let me love her
She made me promise
I was going to love her forever
And forever and forever.
I tried to tell her,
I said, "Look, Honey, let's make a deal
We'll love each other come what will
Til May Day then we'll see what's what.
Anyway, May Day's my birthday
I'm bound to be in a good mood.
We'll renew our little love contract
If we want to and go straight through
Til Christmas."

She wouldn't listen.
So I had to promise to make her
A pair of gold-hooped earrings
From the Moon's disc.
I had to tell her
The devigation of the fireflies
Was nothing compared to her eyes
And silly stuff like that.

When we finished, I took her
To a bar on Broadway.
Her face was still flush with love
But I didn't care,
I had to bare my mind
I had to appear cruel in order to be kind.

"Don't get the wrong idea," I told her
"No matter what I said in bed
I won't be tied down to one woman."

She split her sides laughing.
"Don't tell me you believed that crap,"
She howled, gasping for breath

Like a fish flapping on the sand.
"You're too touching."

She kissed me maternally on the cheek
The way you treat
The idiot of the family
And told me she had to hurry home
Before her husband got there.
Didn't even know she was married.
A few days later
I got to thinking
What a kinky woman she was
And tried to telephone her
But she's given me the wrong number.

In Memorium: Robert Hayden

You read with Auden,
A reading I arranged,
My two male mothers
Side by side
In duel
For my secret soul.

Your hands were weather vanes
Wilting as a young girl's
Ordering orchids.
When the winter
Of discontent
Set in,
They became cracked
And ugly.

Time vindicated
Your fidelity
To craftmanship.
The shrill
Who opposed you
Are silent
As forest at nightfall.

Tell me how do you
Love the waters of death?
Not content to test
With your tippy toes,
You just dived
Right in.

Haki R. Madhubuti

Haki R. Madhubuti was born in 1942. He is the founder of Third World Press and Black Books Bulletin and is one of the world's best-selling authors of poetry and nonfiction. He has published nineteen books, including Black Men: Obsolete, Single, Dangerous? Claiming Earth, *and* Hearts Harvest. *He has edited* Million Man March/Day of Absence: A Commemorative Anthology. *Madhubuti has received numerous awards, among them an American Book Award in 1991. He earned his MFA from the University of Iowa and is professor of English and director of the Gwendolyn Brooks Center at Chicago State University.*

Poet: What Ever Happened to Luther?

he was strange weather, this luther, he read books, mainly poetry and
    sometimes
long books about people in foreign places. for a young man he was too
    serious,
he never did smile, and the family still don't know if he had good teeth. he
    liked
music too, even tried to play the trumpet until he heard the young miles
    davis. He
then said that he'd try writing. the family didn't believe him because there
    ain't
never been no writers in this family, and everybody knows that whatever
    you end
up doing, it's gotta be in your blood. It's like loving women, it's in the
    blood, arteries
and brains. this family don't even write letters, they call everybody. thats
    why
the phone is off 6 months out of a year. Then again, his brother willie T.
    use to
write long, long letters from prison about the books he was reading by
    malcolm x,
frantz fanon, george jackson, richard wright and others. luther, unlike his
    brother,
didn't smoke or drink and he'd always be doing odd jobs to get money.
    even his
closest friends clyde and t. bone didn't fully understand him. while they be
    partying

all weekend, luther would be traveling. he would take his little money with a

bag full of food, mainly fruit, and a change of underwear and get on the greyhound

bus and go. he said he be visiting cities. yet, the real funny thing about luther was

his ideas. he was always talking about africa and black people. he was into that

black stuff and he was as light skin as a piece of golden corn on the cob. he'd be

calling himself black and african and upsetting everybody, especially white people.

they be calling him crazy but not to his face. anyway the family, mainly the educated

side, just left him alone. they would just be polite to him, and every child of god

knows that when family members act polite, that means that they don't want to be

around you. It didn't matter much because after his mother died he left the city

and went into the army. the last time we heard from him was in 1963. he got put

out the army for rioting. he disappeared somewhere between mississippi and

chicago. a third cousin, who family was also polite to, appeared one day and said

that luther had grown a beard, changed his name and stopped eating meat. She

said that he had been to africa and now lived in Chicago doing what he wanted to

do, writing books, she also said that he smiles a lot and kinda got good teeth.

Magnificent Tomorrows

For Queen Mother Moore, Karima White, Sonia Sanchez,
Mari Evans, Ruby Dee, Assata Shukur,
Julia Fields, and Janet Sankey

1.
flames from sun
fire in during rainbow nights.

the women are colors of earth and ocean—
earth as life,
the beginning waters,
magnificent energy.

as the women go, so go the people,
determining mission,
determining possibilities.

stopping the women stops the future.
to understand slavery, feel the eyes of mothers.
there lies hope of destruction, lies unspeakable horror or
fruitful destiny.

we
are now in the europe of our song,
non-melody with little beat or hope.
current dreams are visionless,
producing behavior absent of greatness.

2.
without great teachings,
without important thoughts,
without significant deeds,
the ordinary emerges as accepted example
gluing the women
to kitchens,
afternoon soaps,
and the limiting imagination of sightless men.
producing
a people that move with the
quickness of decapitated bodies
while
calling such movement
divine.

possibilities: listen to the wind of women, the voices of big mama, zora
    neale, sister rosa,
fanny lou, pretty renee, gwen brooks, queen nzinga, and warrior mothers.
    all birth and
prophecy, black and heart warm, bare and precise. the women detailing
    the coming collapse

or rise. the best and bent of youth emerging. telling triumphantly. if
    we listen, if we
feel & prepare.

3.
if black women do not love
there is no love.
if black women do not love,
harmony and sustaining humanity cease.
if black women do not love,
strength disconnects.
families sicken, growth is questionable &
there are few reasons to conquer ideas or foe.

as black women love
europe gives way to southern meals,
as black women mature,
so come flames from sun,
rainbows at dusk,
sculpture of elizabeth catlett and
music of nina simone.
as womenblack connect,
the earth expands, minds open and books reveal the possible
if we study
if we listen,
if we concentrate,
if we carefully care,
if we simply do.

Possibilities: Remembering Malcolm X

it was not that you were pure.
your contradictions were small wheels,
returning to the critical questions:
        what is good?
        what does it mean to be black?
        what is wise?
        what is beautiful?
        where are the women and men of honor?
        what is a moral-ethical consciousness?
        where will our tomorrows be?
        what does a people need to mature?

it was your search and doings
that separated you from puppets.
"a man lives as a man does"

if you lived among the committed
this day how would you lead us?

what would be your strength,
the word, the example, both?

would you style in thousand
dollar suits and false eye glasses?

would you kneel at the feet of arabs
that raped your grandmother?

would you surround yourself with
zombies in bow ties, zombies with parrot tongues?

it was not that you were pure.
the integrity of your vision and pain,
the quality of your heart and decision
confirmed your caring for local people, and your
refusal to assassinate progressive thought
has carved your imprint on the serious.

The Union of Two
For Ife and Jake

What matters is the renewing and long running kinship
seeking common mission, willing work, memory, melody, song.

marriage is an art,
created by the serious, enjoyed by the mature,
watered with morning and evening promises.

those who grow into love
remain anchored
like egyptian architecture and seasonal flowers.

it is african that woman and man join in smile, tears, future.
it is traditional that men and women share expectations, celebrations,
    struggles.

it is legend that the nations start in the family.
it is african that our circle expands.
it is wise that we believe in tomorrows, children quality.
it is written that our vision will equal the promise.

so that your nation will live and tell your stories accurately,
you must be endless in your loving touch of each other, continuance the
    answers.

Bahiyyih Maroon

Bahiyyih Maroon, born in 1973, is a native of New York City. Her work has appeared in FireWater Poetics, The Fuse-A Journal of the Nuyorican Poets Cafe, The New York Times, *and several small New York literary journals and magazines.*

Fire Keeper
For Mumia Abu Jamal—political prisoner

i save your grace inside
pamphlet shrines/   thin books/
the skulls of our dead
i speak to your legend often
and wonder what you think about
pissing on the prison toilet
bleeding your pencil hung words
in exile

You printed the move
exhaling charcoal graffiti
through the narrow tubes of journalism.
dissecting cointelpro strategies into split factions
insisting conspiracy theories at every printing
until they made you a part of one
now, only you can recount your story
one sprawled out on the oil drive
in a bloodied night.
there are casualties
some of whom still breathe
and sweat pus from blindfolded eye jams

you are centered
in this excrement bathed hole
we call America—a periodical
of our new age bondage
the fiber optic chains on your mind
popped open/   your tongue becoming
a finely serrated blade/   you pierce
the lies

sometimes, i dream you
knotty dreads screaming with the tightly blown wind
fire strapped across the backdrop
this is battle
our hands are wet
with the liver and kidney of our tormentors
i see you
hunter truth/   heart of human animal in hand
raging/ AMANDLA! ! !/ AMANDLA! ! !
you dance vicious/ unlocking Winnie
calling a nation of unbordered Zulus to war
and we love/   in this boiled summer/
you 21st. Century warrior in graying locks
redeemer of printed language
you taste the precious finite reality life is/
each these numbered days
knowing death to be inescapable
that injustice feeds on the truism
and plays the chords of our reaper often
in the auditorium of this decorated concentration camp

i see you Mumia
in that flat coal space
running   /   conjure and
write firmly/   in stone/   we will strike matches
against the hemorrhaged visions you bear
and set the cities to drown in our blaze

Nude Womon Spotted in Cappuccino Cup as Advertising Dollar co-opts another life

How does it feel to be
the absolute meaning of chocolate—cafe au lait
to be edible body/   and whole
easily shaved   /   completely swallowed
legs up/   slip spot secrets/   suppositions of pride
stripped between bills and blood
who are you wheat soaked woman?
how do I come to the pistol glare
of your cinnamon sprinkled areola
on the back of slick magazine

compromised of style and laid out
as just another Brown Sunshine girl[1]

you as cliché/   as menu/   dipped
in the creme of a pale cafe/   sellin wears
on your Dkinga[2] grooved body
again
it's givin me the blues/   dammmn
gettin me to blues
again

Neighbor

For Lynn Hoeum

silence
between the floorboards
claims us without asking and
nearly without our knowing

would it have been different?

if from the beginning
your womuness were clear to me—
instead of confused by the wind
black hair sculpting
your shortened torso
the minute long legs
shrinking your breastless frame
until you struck me certainly
as just a girl

would i
have walked more willingly
into foreign air of your family
home, scent of spices repugnant
clung to sweated atmosphere
stirred by half dozen bodies
inhabiting space sized as my own

1. Slang expression meaning prostitute.
2. A Kongo cosmogram indicative of the crossroads of life. Specifically the soul's orbit
of birth/life/death/reincarnation.

and in a way that forces my lover and i
to edges of tension
swayed calm with an uneasy tenderness
as roses unfold
from ill placed sockets

time to learn the uneven path
our languages grating—
halted against eachother
slips down the aisle
with the crisp silk you wear
on this marriage day
ringing as the open seed of dawn

i am left to wonder
what you would have told me
of your first country
the way the landside's
greening flesh was
exaggerated/ forgotten
for a pushed awake city
drowned with bodies
and their perfectly
inconsistent lives
what would you have said of
how my flag ate the meters of
earth and bone from there
how the soprano still screams
shifted above the sunless killing fields
what words
would you have used to tell me
the gross repetition of my questions
aimed at you and having little to do with you
with the moods that curl across your skin
in the mornings—the particular intent of your lips
meeting themselves before the bathroom mirror
each day as you wear further
into the urban still life

which letters would i have grabbed at
to explain the disgrace
of curiosity
without

bridges
or names

my anger in this is plain
what takes you away is a design
an easy graceless pattern laid down
over our bassinets and baskets
these months we have followed our paths
loving above all
the familiarity of
our families, our men
wrapped firmly in the
distinct flags our
tiny worlds hardly deserve
owning little and least of all
ourselves
we belong to something larger
and far less extraordinary
than eachother

Tony Medina

Tony Medina, born in 1966, teaches English at Long Island University's Brooklyn Campus. He is the literature editor of NOBO: A Journal of African American Dialogue. *The author of* No Noose Is Good Noose *and coeditor with S. E. Anderson of* In Defense of Mumia, *his work is featured in the anthologies* In the Tradition, Aloud, *and* Soulfires, *as well as many literary and popular culture publications.*

The Big House Revisited

bigger thomas
wasn't suppose
to make it
to the big house
sippin tea
with Miss Anne
& Sydney Poitier
& Botswana
but he did
& became
a modern day
Mandingo
w/ 3 legs
& small change
& big chains
clamped around
his neck
presupposing the noose
wrapped tight
around his nuts
w/ a media blitz
& crew cut fits
& tears imprisoned
in the slits
of his eyes
& funeral procession
rides with a barrel
to his head
going far
going far

in a car with no wheels
in a plane with no wings
towards a sky with no stars
but one big ass sun
melting his dreams away
on the front page
of a back alley rag
in stereo
with a light
in his face
and a mic
to record
the pace
of his heart
stuck high
in his throat
bigger thomas
wasn't suppose
to make it
to the big house
Not the bigger
from the hood
who was taught
in school
that he would
amount to nothing good
that black was bad
& white was good
the bigger paralyzed
by white supremacy
who smothered Mary Dalton
out of fear
demonized bigger
who was looked at
as ape as rapist
the bigger who bashed
black bessie's face in
with a brick
the bigger that was
trained to be sick
but the bigger
who was smaller
the bigger who was

a belly crawler
a coke bottled pubic haired
shit grinnin shit talkin scab
leaving his sister in a welfare hotel
while he sits twiddling his thumbs
on supreme court benches
with the rest of the out house wenches & henches
& stenches reeking of hypocrisy & injustice
Nor the bigger
who once wrote of ambulances
not comin for niggers tonight
who couldn't play jazz
& became a critic
but was so short
he ended up being
a backward backbiting tic
in the flea collar
of right-wing neo-con twits
always bitter & always wrong
but still
writing notes
for votes
from the white litter rotty
volunteering to be a hanging judge
he hate black so much
he turnin white now
aint karma a bitch!
or the bigger who write for the Daily News
the one who stole Earl Caldwell's job
the one Baraka called a safe knee grow
the one that look & talk like Foghorn Leghorn,
                I SAY!   I SAY!
Not bigger twirling in the air
now swatting Haitian slave labor made balls
with bats after the media assassinated
him after the mob assassinated
him father framing a poor white boy
& bigger
or the bigger twirling on stage
marrying Elvis' daughter
after the press pressed him
into press conferences
to pay for pedophile

dis charges
but the bigger
in bars
where bookstores
& libraries should be
the bigger
behind bars
w/ James Brown
& Mike Tyson
or those babies
we read for in the Bronx
at Spofford
the over 60%
of biggers
who leave their mother's womb
& no sooner pass the corner curb
before getting carted away to jail
on the front page
of the six o'clock news
like yesterday's deposit bottles
cashed in for privatized prisons
& construction contracts
& a reserve army of slave labor
baited by imported crack
& junk & lifestyles
on the silver screen
on the boob tube
& the streets
they call their school
creating jobs
where they don't exist
selling for the man
executing his plan
to execute the poor
who want to obliterate
the memory of their poverty
& bleed workers of their hard work
and illusory sense of stability
to have them feel helpless & unsafe
in their neighborhoods or their homes
blaming youth bitterly criticizing youth
the working class
whose taxes pay

the salaries
of the police
who sweep
our broken youth
off the curb
from selling poor
people herb
where they'll have
a new job
w/ no pay & no benefits
to benefit
the State & capital
psyching out
our youth
to have them
think that
this is what
it takes
to be a man
Nah, bigger thomas
wasn't suppose
to make it
to the big house
w/ Rochester
& Man Tan
w/ Cleotis
& Sir Han Sir Han
workin for the man
to keep the hand
rockin the cradle,
Not bigger
runnin w/ a ball
through airports
or leaving his wife
to snort up white whores
at cocktail parties
w/ Richard Pryor & Jim Brown
back slappin barbies
givin other men head
in their wedding gowns
The bigger they want
gots to put his soul on ice
gots to crave lice

over wife
over life
a shrimp to eat
small fish to fry
that stinks on ice
whose life's a lie
the bigger they want
wants nothin to do
with the hood
the bigger they want
believes black is bad
& white is good
the bigger they want
act silly
& gives big neon plastic smiles
in the movies
on the TV
or at the M.L.A. conference
the bigger they want
gots to be a good
lay
on command
to be able to allow
for the man
to take his hands
off the strings
enough to dip
into his stash
bigger can't have chump change
bigger is chump change
bigger is chump
bigger don't want change
in Capitalist America
the bigger they want
be on Time magazine
with a penciled in
five day growth
straddled atop the Empire State Building
swatting helicopters like flies
never letting go
he white woman
bigger thomas
wasn't suppose

to make it
to the big house
sippin tea
with Miss Anne
& Sydney Poitier
& Botswana
Nah, bigger thomas
wasn't suppose
to make it
to the big house
bigger thomas
was born
there
& he will
die there
if he don't really mature
and change into the man
he's suppose to be
without strings
attached
bein everybody's
big tom

October 10, 1994
Harlem, New York

After the Verdict

When the verdict
was read
& O.J. was acquitted
Black people cheered
While White people jeered,

Their faces glum & pale
unlike the ones found
flashing their blood-stained
teeth
in the photos
of lynchings.

E. Ethelbert Miller

E. Ethelbert Miller, born in 1950, is the director of the African American Resource Center at Howard University. He is the author of Where Are the Love Poems for Dictators? *(1986) and* First Light: Selected and New Poems *(1994). He is also the editor of* In Search of Color Everywhere, *which was awarded the 1994 PEN Oakland Josephine Miles Award.*

My Father's Girlfriend

in
New York
my mother opens
her apartment door
after several knocks

her face
reminds me of Alberta
Hunter the year she
came out of retirement

in her eyes
something my father
fell in love with

You Send Me: Bertha Franklin, December 11, 1964

What am I suppose to do
when the Devil comes knocking?
I pray to Jesus for protection
but I keep a gun like a blanket
for cold air and strange men.

Folks say I shot Sam Cooke
tonight but it was an angry man
I killed. I didn't hear any music
when he died, just the screams of
a young woman running from the
room next door. Her hands holding
the pants of love.

the night before the first
day of school

the night before the first
day of school. the house as
quiet as when i lived alone.
the cool summer air ending
as i breathe in the night.
during these moments of
fatherhood i count my black
blessings. i leave this poem
on the table next to the
lunch bags and books.

Players

When Mickey Mantle died
I saw myself once again
jumping against a fence
in the South Bronx, the
ball coming to rest in
my glove. My own centerfield
as large as the housing
projects so many could
not escape.

The Boys of Summer

Carlton, Patrick and I
are waiting for autographs
outside Yankee Stadium. The summer
of 1960 and Mazeroski has not hit
the homerun which will break our
hearts. We are years away from
memories, our wives and our children.
On this day we see Mickey Mantle coming
to work, his uniform of stripes waiting
inside. We run to catch "The Mick" to
have him sign his name on whatever we
own. Our lives sheltered from segregation.

Our mothers talking about Jackie Robinson
and how Willie Mays learned to catch a ball
while turning his back, running full speed
as if he was Emmett Till.

Lenard D. Moore

Lenard D. Moore was born in 1958 and raised in Jacksonville, North Carolina. A graduate of Shaw University, he has published poetry in more than three hundred magazines, newspapers, and anthologies, such as African American Review, The Pittsburgh Quarterly, Callaloo, Modern Haiku, *and* Obsidian II. *A resident of Raleigh, his books include* The Open Eye, Forever Home, *and* Desert Storm: A Brief History.

The Song Poem

I will sing in the rising
of wind, the warming
of sun, and peeling
of skin—will sing
of pain, the wailing,
the swelling, the blood
strumming sun-colored notes.

I am song, to the woman,
when the river floods
in my manhood.
I am black song,
blasting stern language
from a deep heart
in the morning light.

I hear the currents surge
and rhythm, pitch by pitch,
in the flow of my blood.
I am the song's note of wind,
the pain oozing from the throat,
a chord tuning its scale:
harmony itself, itself.

Gifts

That Christmas, unlike others,
my father was gone, though he wrote letters,

and sent my mother money
to buy five sons and two daughters gifts
like a good father would, like the good one
that he still is, in his ripening age.

Vietnam came on like a nightmare,
then festered and burst like a sore.
My father experienced.
We were silent when he came back.
The jungles and rice paddies
are still wet in his eyes.

My football waited under the silvery tree
for us to spiral.
Three bicycles sparkled there too.
He would have watched us ride them,
though we kept him in mind
while happily jumping over homemade ramps.

His favorite chair was empty
and as cold as a vacant room.
Still it was Christmas to us.
We munched apples and oranges.
My mother cuddled each one of us
as if we were teddy bears.

Christmas went that way
until my father returned
to the land he knew acre by acre
no matter how bare the trees,
how grassless the earth seemed
that Christmas now pressed
in an album of photographs.

I was only twelve,
searching for my father
to spread the news to him
like a messenger,
that he wasn't there
when the gifts were opened.

Haiku

cloudless summer day—
pitching pennies against the wall
the street musician

Haiku

Spring moonrise—
behind the blues singer
cymbals trembling

Haiku

Family reunion—
smoke from the grilling steak
drifts on noonday heat

Tanka

month of rain ends—
hoeing tomatoes for my father
this breezeless day
my cousin waves from rank weeds
and an ambulance passes

Tanka

after church meeting
grandma dumps cornbread batter
in the shiny pan—
the smell of collard greens
lingering on summer air

Jalaluddin Mansur Nuriddin

Jalaluddin Mansur Nuriddin, born in 1944, is the mainstay of the poetry ensemble/recording artists The Last Poets. His poetry is featured on eight Last Poets' albums: The Last Poets, This Is Madness!, Chastisement, At Last, Delights of the Garden, Oh My People, Freedom Express, *and* Scatterap/Home. *Jalal has also recorded the solo albums* Doriella Du Fontaine, The Hustler's Convention, *and* On the One. *Some of his early poetry was recorded under the names "Lightnin Rod" and Alafia Pudim. Selected poems are printed in* Vibes from the Scribes.

Children of the Future

Now the children of the future tried to come to terms
with the industrialized nations and their corporate firms

To decontaminate the planet and meet their demands
detoxify the oceans, rivers, lakes, and lands

Purify the air, get rid of nuclear waste
put it on a rocket ship and send it into space

Tone down, bone down, hone down hatred
'til love for the Most High's creation was sacred

Rectify, recompense, reevaluation
clarify, satisfy the present situation

Spiritualize, realize, crystallize aspirations
recognize, stabilize the unity of nations

chorus

Take all the bullshit and bury it with a shovel
quit the lying, spying, alibiing, darin' the devil

But the parents of the future, like the ones in the past
had an apocalyptic childhood and the dye was cast

Those among their leaders were the children of the present
diabolical, devious, and extremely unpleasant

163

chorus

Irradiated, mutated, DNA deranged
SCI-FI, sinister, slick and strange

In a megalomaniac, satanic, pseudo scientific mode
at the pavilion of oblivion based on creed and code

The super secret, clandestine, indiscreet elite
saw their conquest of nature ending in defeat

They had dared to do what they shouldn't have done
and the planet overheated from the rays of the sun

You couldn't tell them nothing 'cause they didn't want to hear it
and were oppressing all the people 'til they just couldn't bear it

So the children of the future went underground
so deep down that they couldn't be found

Fleeing for their lives for all it was worth
they burrowed in their capsules 'til they reached the third earth

chorus

At a depth that was equal to the stratosphere
They met the underground dwellers who lived down there

These subterraneans were evolved and aware of the facts
and gave the children shelter then covered their backs

They were illuminated, elevated, extra-sensory heightened
transcendental, mega-mental, fully enlightened

chorus

Into teleportation, levitation, meditation, cryptographics
clairvoyance, telekinetics, astral travel, telepathics

Comprehensive comprehension, total memory retention
in every third eye–seeing subterranean super being
within a multiple dimension gravitational suspension

Then they taught all the children about the secrets of life
to gain inner peace instead of stress and strife

Meanwhile the mutated fabricated tyrants and such
were trying to colonize space but it was mega-too much

Their computers were deluders, and androgenous clones
had the planet subdivided into no-go zones

chorus

With their doomsday scenarios all coming to pass
they were holding out in dread and doubt until the last

While the pursuit of the children had been in vain
with everything to lose and nothing to gain

Making war on the surface time and time again
'til the end was beginning, from beginning to end

chorus

But the children of the future had learned the arts
in unity of mind, body, spirit and hearts

They kept on evolving 'til they reached the stage
when the children of the future finally came of age

For death had taught them what life was worth
and had prepared them for the task of leaving planet earth

chorus

Then a starship came down from deep within outer space
and took the children of the future to join the cosmic race.

Dominique Parker

Dominique Parker was born in 1964 in Haiti and raised in Queens, New York. She graduated from New York University law school but decided to write poetry rather than practice law. She is currently a graduate student in the MFA program at Syracuse University.

Foxfire
For Nadja 1962–1992

I imagine her couplings and uncouplings,
the slam of flesh on flesh trying to create a spark:
How she walked
the rounded smoothness of her immobility
the sweat heat smell of her on Garden Street.
No one told her and she didn't know she could offer more
than the open beauty of her thighs.

Her thirty years spent preparing for this ending.
Transformation consumes her cell by cell
her skin becomes the bark of a burial tree.

Last week, she began to glow faintly,
a kindling pile propped in a hospital bed.
Near her door a nurse said, "facemasks"
like a greeting.

She used to wear her light skin and dark eyes
with the ease of peaches
just before teeth break the skin and chew flesh.
Now she is darkened wood
refusing to be consumed by fire
yield to change, become charcoal.
I thought the masks were to protect us
from the taste of her burning ash.

Later, there will be no flame,
no incandescent burst, no brightening.
She will wilt down to darkness—
burn of memory, faint gleam of bone.

Sand

On October 25, 1994, in South Carolina, a white woman,
Susan Smith, alleged that a black man forced her
out of her car at gunpoint, and drove away with her
two small sons still in the car. Police are investigating.

Our story didn't make the six o'clock news. The other story did. The one
about the little white boys, innocent victims, carried away by a dark
stranger. Still, we were arrested, Butch and me, after work on a
Wednesday. Butch was trying to figure out how many thousands of yards
of white broadcloth he'd have to make at the mill, before he had enough
money for school. Laughing, he walked down the street. The sound just
rippled out of him, sliding along the flex of his chest muscles. A carload
of deputies pulled up next to us on the street. Shouting, they bee-
swarmed out and surrounded us: Don't move! Don't move! They pushed
me face down on the car hood. With my cheek pressed to the metal, still
warm from the engine, I concentrated on looking harmless, law-abiding.
They pulled my arms behind my back. Butch had to lie on the sidewalk.
He didn't fight, at nineteen, he knew the drill. They patted our arms,
between our legs, searching for weapons. I could feel the eyes of the
people behind the store windows, judging us. Deciding we were
kidnappers, maybe murderers. We were the last two of thirty-five men
placed in the large cell. The walls were scratched with messages and
phone numbers. One wall was thick metal bars. It smelled of old piss and
new sweat. Nobody looked like anybody else. Though mostly we were
tall and brown. A lot were young. Butch tried not to look scared. I
wanted to hold him, tell him, everything was gonna be allright, say—
Daddy'll protect you, but I couldn't. There was nothing I could say to
my boy. In the corner one man in a suit began to complain, loud. He
looked like he worked behind a desk in a bank or insurance office. The
Sheriff questioned us one at a time. When a deputy took Butch away I
tried to explain his innocence: He's saving money for college. My turn.
Across from the Sheriff in a room with no windows, I stared into his eyes
and thought about being tired. The Sheriff asked me if I had anything to
say in my defense. Well, on the day I was born, God was sick . . . This is
not a fucking joke. If we don't find those boys one of you could get the
chair. Back in the cell Butch wouldn't meet my eyes. He stared off, and
his hard manface promised he was leaving. But, where could he go?
North? To live with our people in Boston? After a while they told us we
were free to leave, and I tried to get used to the way the ground moved
under my feet. Even after they let us go I could feel the not-quite-

firmness of it. How we were walking on solid ground, then, it shifted,
gave way a little and suddenly everywhere we stepped was sand.

The Art of the Nickname

RULE: It is important not to wear out the freshness and original taste of
        a person's
name through overuse

(If your name is Beatrice you will be called BeBe)

The claim is nicknames are created because there are children. Children
        name
themselves or their brothers and sisters by choosing a word they can say.
        Somehow
it is proof you are loved; preserving the slurred half pronounced
        utterances. This
ignores the capriciousness of the parental element. The moment of leaning
        over the
crib, basket, or blanket. The parent's mouth shaping the nameword.

If you are a boy you will be called Pichon—this is a plant disease. If you
        are a girl
you will be called Peaches—these are fruit. If you are a boy you will
        be called Papi—
this is the Father. If you are a girl you will be called Poulette—this is a
        chicken. If
you are a child you will be called Mama, Poupette, Peanut, Junior, Niecey,
        or
Littleman. These are nonnegotiable.

RULE: Caricature should not be confused with nicknaming.

(If your name is Barbara you will be called Buffie)

If you are five and cannot eat a plate of black-eye peas out of fear—a
        thousand
disembodied eyes staring at you—you will be called the girl who wouldn't
        eat her
food. This is temporary and meaningless.

If you go to the Mother's house she will find a name for you. If you
    go only once or,
are a stranger, the name will say what is remembered about you.

(If your name is Kyle you will be called Pookie)

No one liked BigheadWanda. Naming her was a way to remind ourselves
    of our
dislike and to keep it from softening to pity. FatblackKaren was different.
    At first,
it was how we remembered she was not a friend. After a while we realized
    she was
smart and one of us. Then, we said it softer, with respect, but
    absent-minded; the
way we said Fred when we meant casual fuck, or Sharon when we meant
    living
alone.

(If your name is Richard you will be called Butchie)

RULE: Nicknaming is not just a shortening of someone's name. (If your
    name is
Eldridge you will be called Skipper) Nicknaming requires individual
    effort and
creativity.

If you go to the Mother's house and are part of the group you will get
    a nickname.
Whim is important. You can have more than one because more than one
    person is
seeing and naming you. The names should be reactive and interactive—the
nickname of the nickname.

Sometimes, when a stranger asks the Mother her name and she doesn't
    want to tell it
she says, "Cathy." This is not a nickname. This is an alias.

COROLLARIES:

If you tell lies you will be called poet
If you are smug you will be called intellectual
If you love women you will be called dyke
If you love men you will be called fag

If you love power you will be called patriot
If you are Black you will be called nigger
If you come from an island you will be called coconut
If you are light-skinned you will be called redbone
If you are dark-skinned you will be called tarbaby
If you are too smart you will be called white
If I dislike you I will call you trifling
If I disrespect you I will call you ho
If we are friends I will call you girl
If we are friends I will call you boy
If we fight I will call you stupidfuck
If you are unknown I will call you the folks
If you are unknown I will call you whitefolks
If I know you I will call you by your name
If you know me you will know my name

When Mark Deloach Ruled the World

> *. . . your hair's so nappy who in the world is your
> pappy you sho' is one ugly child . . .*

It was Summer, all the time;
the street of South Ozone
crackled, the sound of playing cards
slapping the spokes of bicycle wheels;
Only one rule to remember, avoid
any places you might meet Mark.
He was not from the neighborhood.
Though we knew there were many
DeLoachs, only his hard stare
forced a name into our mouths.
Behind his back we were brave,
singing songs about him being bug-ugly,
peasyheaded, poor; Saying we weren't scared.
Still, anytime he could stop us
one, three, five of us, take whatever he wanted,
beat down whoever he felt looked at him wrong.
We knew it was better to get out of the way.
Accepted his meanness, adjusted,
the way we jumped our fences afternoons
when Ali let out his wild dog,
for its run down the block.

We never told anyone, we saw him
on the over pass, above the Van Wyck expressway,
cars streaming below,
collection of bottles at his feet, we knew
and we ran, didn't wait to see
the cylinders rocket from his palm,
end over end, arcing high
then tumbling down.

Eugene B. Redmond

Eugene B. Redmond, born in 1937, has authored six volumes of poetry and has received numerous awards, including a National Endowment for the Arts Creative Writing Fellowship, a Pushcart Prize, and an American Book Award in 1993 for his most recent volume, Eye in the Ceiling. A native of East St. Louis, he is Professor of English at Southern Illinois University, Edwardsville, and the founding editor of Drumvoices Revue.

Milestone: The Birth of an Ancestor
For Miles Dewey Davis, III
(1926–1991)
in Memoriam, in Futuriam

Prologue

Dressed up in pain
the flatted-fifth began its funeral climb
up the tribal stairwell:

grief-radiant as it
bulged and gleamed with moans
spread like laughter or Ethiopia's wings
mourned its own percussive rise
became blue-borne
in the hoarse East Saint Louis air;

bore witness to the roaring calm
the garrulous silence
the caskets of tears
the gushing stillness:

the death of the Cool
became the birth of an Ancestor.

Gwensways
For Gwendolyn Brooks

Cautious & Incantatory
Proverbial & Incremental
Kinetic & Incendiary

She Languages down
   Un-illuminated
   Avenues
   Of The inflated
   The sleepwoke
   The impish   The august   The possessed
   The disengaged   The emblematic   The ugly

Wearing her—
   make you wanna hiss/make you wanna hush
—verbal amulets
Like crosses;

   Pith
   Parchment and
   Prophecy
Fly from this intersperser of Dread-Words;

   O, the ways of our
   Wise counterclock woman!

Momenting the Ancestrail:
Evocative, uneclipsed, evangelical:

   Intricate: Intimate:
   Her Call/Our Response
   Continuum.

Aerolingual Poet of Prey

For Alvin Aubert who surveys
Life from the quiet's deep see.

Through a two-way telescope of time,
he tracked the stormy calms of history.
Carried gravity in his sight. Behind
him stretched a flapping scroll of ir-
reconcilable callings. Before, there
swirled a grinning turret of racial
daggers aiming to splinter the brother-
ing father within him. From gooberdust
rainlore graphite redbeans gut-trails
creole-dreams ink river korean-conflict

mardi-gras typewriter bible nightmare
ritual-rice and computer he forged wings
of discovery wings/of delivery. Gained
griot-height. And orbiting gave birth
to *Obsidian.*

Became poet of prey:
South Louisiana aero-linguist. Resur-
rected life's raw incenses. Re-forged
cool wordbolts. Moved North: Leaned
South. Kept *Feeling Through.* Kept com-
ing smack up *Against the Blues.* Kept
planting earthharp in air.

> In-flight, he drank his brew
> of laments: *trouble-deep rivers*
>   *river-deep troubles*

> In-flight, *skimmed fear off death.*

Poet of prey:
Scavenger who claimed and climbed language.
Rocked and groaned through love's highlow.
Closed: Opened in the moontime of need. Follow-
ed quick/eccentric dartings. Entered slow/blood-
filled hiding places. Lusted after sizzling carry-
overs. Twitched in the rumble-quiet: In the
sweat-time of riots. Watched the glitter of
upheaval grow sheenless in the logic of
darklight. Wrote. Wished. Salivated. Stayed
Case. Stayed edge. Stayed course.

Poet of prey:
Proper poppa chronicler. Lured concentric
florals of grief into slim sleeves of poetry.
Into rural sheaths of jubilant anger: Into
lyrics of coiled, knowledgeable passion.
Into folk-lucid tropes. Holy-evil. Grimace. Twist.

Poet of prey:
Hear his sober ecstacies resonate. See

them levitate midst the heart's acoustics.
Alvin Aubert: clear, spicy, bright babble
made edible as in a gulp of blues. Inhalable
as in the first pungent breeze of gumbo.

Ishmael Reed

Ishmael Reed, born in 1938, is an Oakland-based writer who has written more than twenty books across several genres. In addition to novels, plays, and essay collections, his work includes the poetry volumes Catechism of D Neoamerican Hoodoo Church, A Secretary to the Spirits, Chattanooga, Conjure, *and* New & Collected Poems. *Recipient of numerous honors, fellowship, and prizes, Reed teaches at the University of California at Berkeley.*

I am not the walrus

I am not the walrus
I am the virus
your insides are my supper
you are defenseless against me
your science impotent
your antibiotics
I trick them
I am not the walrus
I am the virus
Wipe that smile off your face
this is serious
I can make you delirious
spending all of your
waking hours in the can
Nobody can give you a hand
I am not the walrus
I am the virus
I can render you incapable
of eating
of loving
When I get finished with you
You will curse the day you
were born
Your mother, your father
Your god cannot help you
I spit on your god
I will make you hot all over
I will send you chills
Your bills will pile up

You will bleed from every
hole in your body
O, you think that I am
ugly
Just for that I will
pock up your pretty face
You will put food into
your throat path
I will block the path
Population control
Get out of the way
I'll show you how
to deal with that
Your body will shrink
like a popped balloon
I will follow you into the
ground
I will fight the worms
Over you
You are mine
You belong to me
I am not the walrus
I am the virus

El Paso Monologue

Mexico needs mahogany
and I plan to sell it to them
They're too far north to have
their own
It's not as cold as
it is in Yucatan
New Guinea
50 degrees year around
My men can't go swimmin
Lots of elk and deer
because we killed off
their natural enemies
Bears and panthers
Bobcats aren't strong
enough to get rid of them
The lakes have sunk

twenty feet and so
because they can't hide
from the birds
the fish supply has
been depleted
I'd like to set up

some businesses in
Russia
They have the most
trees outside of South
America
But nobody knows what's
going to happen there
Those people are like
The woodpeckers who
leave holes in our trees
Absolutely no concept
of private property

Samuel F. Reynolds

Samuel F. Reynolds, born in Buffalo, New York, in 1967, is a writer and theater artist based in Philadelphia. His essays and poetry have been included in several publications, including Negative Capability, Voices: How Our Ancestors Speak, *and* Testimony: Young African-Americans on Self-Discovery and Black Identity.

moon/light quarter/back sack

The calico summer
dress sheathed
the woman warrior. Undone,
she gleamed
brighter than the moon.
Her skin, flourescent gray.
Her sweat gathered
on me like dew.
She skewered me
to turf
with my own weapon.
The Earth started drumming
my mind.
I tried to stand but
just lifted my head
to see her
riding me into battle.

The Whipping

I ran,
from what, I didn't remember.
Until my mangled foot,
stumbled over a dead body,
pale by death and birth.
The long, thick, black whip,
still held in his death clutch,
was wrapped around his narrow neck.
His bulging, empty blue eyes told
of the terror his swollen, blue tongue

in his gaping mouth
never would.
I ripped the whip away from his neck
like thread on a spool.
A small trickle of dark blood oozed
from his broken flesh.
With blood in my eye and my old trainer in hand,
I began to beat him
again
and again, for every
eye that saw me lose my shame by his hand
again, for every
sip of lemonade in the shade
again, for every
drop of sweat I drank in the midday sun
again, for every time
he called me "Boy!" and my son came too
again, for every time
he patted my daughter's ass and my wife's too
again, for
patting my ass
again, for every time
his bitch wife came near me when she was in heat
again, for every
sore on my tongue from biting it,
again, for every
minute I was chained like beast in a lair
again, for
never saying thank you
again, for
never . . . remembering my birthday
and again. . . .
for being my father and creator
and again. . . .
for choking him to death and still running away.

With each crack of the leather
I felt the whip recoil further around
my shoulder,
my neck,
my mind,
my heart,
so I stopped.

What was willfully forgotten was remembered
and willfully to be forgotten again.

Now,
gratefully,
gracefully,
I walk
whirling the whip above my head
to create,
from fleeting wisps of air fleeting
through hard
blood-stained leather,
the wind music
to call forth my chorus,
my children,
my heart,
my mind,
my Self.

An Open Letter to All Black Poets

*All Black poets who use "Black" in their poems should be
taxed five dollars.—Mat Johnson, novelist and friend.*

You be tellin' me You Be Black
Blu Black, Po' Black, So Black, Too Black
Mo' Black, Coal Black, Crazy Black, All Black

It like you be braggin' you humble
It like you be secretly learnin' God's name and then be shoutin' it off da
     rooftops.
It like you be tellin' me to wake up and you be Rip Van Winkle
It like you be shoutin you crazy and then tryin to be my shrink
But how you be tellin' me this?
I was told those who know, don't talk
and those who don't know, be tellin' all their bizness
Don't you know thyself

be tellin' me
you be Shaka, fierce mass murderer of his own, AKA
punk-ass Artie who got new with inner-city flava after spendin' his whole
life blunted by suburbia.

you be Ayo, Yoruba for joy, AKA
Gail who ain't felt no joy since she ran away from Daddy when Daddy
was tryin' to be her Man.

you be Osiris, ancient dickless king of da underworld, AKA
Tony who changed his name to match his fly, fake African gear.
That be the case his name shoulda been J. C. Penney before.

you be Fatima, faithful wife of the prophet, AKA
Stacey who'll get on all-fours for a brother with a little 'erb and some
roughneck rage.

you be Musa, rich and generous Songhai king, AKA
Butch who still be stickin'-up kids 'round da way to get a 40.

You be tellin me this

But
really you be dreaded scott runaway messiahs hanging on rhetorical
     crosses,
until the fire-next-time becomes the inevitable—a real job.

you be thinkin'
yo' phone be tapped
while you be talkin' about how many revolutions you gonna make in her
kinky nation

you be thinkin'
you got secret knowledge
dat the white man paid for you to get in college—
cuz you asked him to.

you be thinkin'
you original man
But how many more of YOU we got to see
before someone realizes you all cut from the same copy.
A stagolee-african prince-revolutionary-intellectual wanna-be

he
—da too Black poet—
be
a punk
                    still
and she be too

She be Sojourner Truthless
gone Hail Mary, mother of Black God-crazy
She be a runaway ghetto Queen who can't rule her mind or body.
She be askin' you to make love to her mind
but if she knew where it was
you be still tryin' to penetrate her hymen of Blame and Pain.
She be tellin' you to "come home" when you be with a white woman
but not be there when you do.
She be weavin her mad-drama Afrocentric romance
in Victorian bedtime story form.
She be the one tellin' me I dissed all Black women in this poem 'cuz
she be thinkin' she an all-Black woman.
She be played and passin' herself off as new.

Truth be
too-Black poets
pop off too much
about they be Black

What else do you be?

Carl Hancock Rux

Carl Hancock Rux, born in 1967, has published work in several anthologies of poetry, drama, and fiction. A resident of Brooklyn, New York, Rux was featured at the 1994 Berlin Jazz Festival and has been commissioned to write poetry for several dance companies, including the Alvin Ailey American Dance Company.

suite repose

I think Archie Shepp played hambone hambone where you been in our living room the night faces & fists melded mellifluous melancholy madness onto red river carpeting—spurt, splash, torrent falls, gushing reds, primeval screams crashing through vodka spittle, sharp tenor sax and subjective alto, trumpet, trombone, hambone bass and Roger Blank drums . . . blank . . . drums . . . blank . . . Shepp's lyricism lurking behind ficus and forlorn fruit and rhythm patterns lined in gold fringe, clutched, clutched in, in our living room, in, where you been arrangements scattered from kidney shaped cherry wood coffee table and camels sleeping in red river woven carpeting, caravans of camels and *Kools* and vodka and blood and Shepp and rhythm . . . I think Garvey's Ghost came to play with me between Charlie Brown sheets to the percussion of belt buckle slaps and cracked wall mirrors and ripped chinese watercolors, or was it Mendacity, either way, the party was in my pillow, where cut outs held court with Right On! magazine centerfolds, conversation was had, freely and maybe Junior Walker interrupted for a moment, or might have been, then again, I think, it was . . . no, yes, it was Mendacity, it was Abbey Lincoln who sent herself into my restlessness and jazz frenzy and comic book high, and quivering and quake and not sure now what the silences mean after Johnnie Walker Black Black Black came crashing down to the harmonic freedom and improvisation of Roach and Mingus and Hawkins and Dizzy . . . Dizzy . . . Dizziness . . .

I know Jimmy Garrison summoned a nature boy to come my way, we entertained battering and long fingernails broke against leather strap, against cheek and ass and eye, I played to Jimmy Garrison's plucking, sucking my thumb in corner circle rhythm patterns, Brilliant Corners, creative post bop, Monk's Brilliant Corners a hiding place, while ass whoopins are taking place, like what seven year old's like me supposed to get for stealing or lying or the kind maybe you hear women who can sing "I Fall In love too Easily" get, who can hang tough with "Willow Weep For Me," and take a swing, take a swing, a swing and a hard hitting fast blow down crashing fruit and floral patterns and primeval screams through vodka spittle, the kinda ass whoopin' maybe women who sing supposed to get after they done tried to do "Afro Blue" but you don't hear about broken nails and Jimmy Garrison and split lip and Eric Dolphy and swollen cheeks against red river roads where camels and cools caravan away from cherry wooded areas, spilling themselves away, like the long and vibrant notes of Yardbird Suite, with the sweet repose of Holiday on "There Is No Greater Love,"

in your living room, jamming, jamming, jamming, they don't tell you about this in record jackets, what to expect when Booker Little sings on that trumpet, when Carlos Valdez gets to cong, cong, congaing, the beat, to beat, to beat, the beat, the beating taking place in the circle of frenzy, in your living room, and there are no sequins for this diva, no boas, no rhinestone tiara, no pencil black eyebrows arched in pride across her forehead, or gentle shadows softly sleeping above the lid of her falling eye, her falling eye in sweet repose, no straightened hair illuminating lights and gels and gobbos, not in your livingroom, just Charles Tolliver's "Plight" to her modern dance ballet, *rond-dé-jam* of the knee, to the fall, to the fist, straight back, and lip split side turn, ever so gracefully, ever so soft, and hard, and swing, and bop, and bam, and pow, and Dizzy . . . dizzy . . . swelling cheeks, weak alto sax, strong bass, I think it was Etta James screaming James . . . james . . . JAMES . . . JAMES JAMES JAMES or maybe the not, or maybe it was just the rustling of the knees and elbows, and the match stick struck across the board, and embers, and smoke rising, and flames, lifting broken body beaten like how, beaten the way seven year olds like me supposed to be beat, or maybe if you Abby Lincoln and sing that good, maybe if you can do primeval screams to Max's drums,

and then there was nothing there . . . and then nothing . . . no voice . . . somebody hollered one last time and I can't recall if it was Grachan Moncur with Sonny Rollins, and Joe Henderson, but I think maybe it was the silences, and Moncur's "Intellect" that came up next, in our living room, with nothing there . . . no voice . . . I think it was the silences . . . finger turning rotary dial . . . door shut . . . locked . . . running water . . . or was it? . . . no, I'm sure it was Moncur . . . who played with me . . . unveiled trombone taking me up in gentle long notes and tickling vibes, texture and shape, and safe brilliant corners to suck

my thumb . . . I think it was the silences . . . next . . . I think it was the
silences.

Pledge of Allegiance

On the first day
I was told a lie
and believed the lie
and liked the lie
and I asked for the truth
but was not given the truth
so I took the lie
and danced with
the lie
footstomped and jigabooed
with the lie
learned to love the lie
and the lie was good
and the lie
was perfect
in lieu of the truth
because i did
not
want to know
the truth
could not face the
truth
i was told the
truth
but did not know the
truth
there's a difference
but then the lie grew
old
and the lie got
bent
and the lie
leaned
and smell'ded
thinskinn'ded
stank up my room
and people

saw right thru
my lie
so i made up
a lie
my own lie
and this lie was
decorative and well dressed
this lie was funny
kept me laughing
this lie was ostentatious
even
colorful and creative
original
I showed off this lie
made love to this lie
and the love was
a lie all its own
wore this lie under my
skirt
let it peek out
every now and then
but that lie got fat
so i made a lie
that was
frail and thin
made me cry
to look at that lie
and everyone
cried for me
weeped at the elegies of
this lie
till that lie regurgitated
till the next lie got
pregnant
with lies
and gave birth
prematurely
contracted and gave
death
so on the second day I thumb painted . . .
i thought I was good
at making lies
but the truth

phoned me at work
titillated my waking hours
bamboozled my dreams
said the lie
lay
listless
and silent
the truth was loquacious
said the lie
was stultifying
and I recalled I
had been told the truth
didn't like the truth
or want to know the
truth
i was told the truth
after I was told
the lie
and then it
was too late
to believe the truth
after you've believed
the lie
and liked the lie
No I did not want to know the
moved south to get away from the
traveled far to forget the
asked Jesus
asked erzuile
asked Vygotsky
to help me mask the
asked the truth to
sit still
be quiet
lay wait
just not be
to be
to was
and on the third day I breathed
I'm finished
and the truth anointed
I am
and I

plié
arabesque
attitude
double kick
jigaboo
to the truth
to be to
be
to am
to know
to is
straight
no chaser
opened my house
to the
evicted the
lie
moved north to nullify
the
changed my name so I couldn't
be recognized by
the
asked Entertainment Tonite
to help me forget
the
cuz I do not know know
no I do not know no
I've heard of
but never met the
don't want to
hear the
will shake hands with
but will not
sit down and
sup with
no
I don't know no
don't care to know
the
truth

Richard Rykard

Richard Rykard, born in 1964, lives in Philadelphia and is a member of the Philadelphia Writers Organization. Also a fiction writer and essayist, his work explores the myth of the emotionally reticent African American male.

A whole two weeks after The Million Man March; and still, if you'd ask me, this is all I could say about it . . .

I marveled at the sight of you who without knowing;
came home, lent freely of yourselves . . . to me.

And I stood back to where the immensity of you stood in a bold,
black relief against the adamant whiteness of the Capitol
building.

I heard prayers and hymns; I witnessed protestations, thought
for a moment; that I saw gods come out from exile behind trees,
from within stone pillars; gods of the bushes, and gods of the
air; to thank us for not forsaking them.

And . . .

In liberation regalia a scruffy Rastafarian palms Bob Marley's
photograph. Mouths in rhythmic contemplation: Jah Rasta Fari.
I thought I saw . . . The Lion of Judah . . .
perched vigilantly on the graying branches of his dreadlocks
watching the crowd and winking, welcoming the company of the
graying black panther just in front of him wishing that Huey
or Eldridge or Fred or Elaine could see him now.

See all these brothers actin right.

I was hugged and my hand was grasped by the man who could not
take his eyes off a bell tower. He was saying:

Surveillance, brother, is how I earned my living
for a lot of years. Now look; you see the window

190

up there; the way it keeps opening and closing,
now . . . why do you think that is?

I was hugged and my hand was grasped by the man who balanced
a small boy on his shoulder. The eyes of the man moist with
tears that came reluctantly as the darkening clouds that
threatened rain; but gave in instead to the burgeoning sunlight.
The eyes of the small boy were wide with wonder and with thrill;
surveying from atop his moutain; a wide black sea.

And then . . . ?

We took to wandering the grounds; made it to the streets, where
black women looked at us; positioned their bodies so we could
see them among the pedestrians, and remind ourselves why we
were there.

and then we stopped to talk to a group of brothers when

Rufus Harley drew in a great breath and blew bagpiped jazz in
the presence of a troupe of drummers who lounged against a grassy
hill.

A man made a face of great exasperation; as he navigated his
daughter's unruly and continuously bobbing head.

Baby you got ta' stay still now, I 'aint
that sure 'bout this braid thang; but
your head gettin' to look a little bad here
now.

Dancers danced in a long ago Africa kicking dust from their
feet and coaxing words from drums; the skins stretched tight
and booming an Ibo, Ife, Yoruba, Ashante reply to the hardened
hands smeared with blood.

I thought I saw

Shaka conferring with Hannibal, and Nzinga; that warrior woman
on horseback; striding through the faces of the women there,
Gospel music roared and tumbled; its ferocity of purpose echoing
the tall ships ferrying rum
molasses

sugarcane and
African huddled masses when their
Veins bulged in necks like rope when a head was thrown back
and a mouth thrown open in celebration of songs of the long
ago.

Saw Booker T. making peace with DuBois, can you believe it?

when they saw that they were both right that day; saw the
talented tenth embracing their more industrially labored cousins.
The souls of black folk
rising
up from slavery

No invisible men here, with no name in the street.

Brothers smiled at me
                    sisters and fathers and the
children of fathers

Looked at me in relief
                    bold black relief.
And we were there, in that place; at that time of an uncommon
commonality we held hands and prayed, each in their own and
to their own.
And I swore I heard Baldwin's Mister Charlie Blues:

> Richard, you can't start walking around believing
> that all the suffering in the world is caused by
> white folks . . .

Kalamu ya Salaam

Kalamu ya Salaam was born in 1947. A New Orleans writer, he was the Louisiana State Literature Fellow for 1995. He is author of eight books of poetry and is editor of Word Up: Black Poetry of the 80s from the Deep South. His latest book of poetry is Cosmic Deputy (1996) and his latest spoken word recording is My Story, My Song (1996).

New Orleans Haiku

French Quarter Intimacies

through weathered wood dark
on shadowed streets ancient voices
whisper history

New Orleans Rainbow

from buttered gold to
purpled black, the sundry shades
of my people shine

Everywhere You Eat

sautéed, baked or fried
this whole hot city is the
kitchen of the gods

Our Natures Rise

hard core nights are so
erotic, a whiff of the
breeze is narcotic

Funeraled Fare Well

we dance in death's face,
send new ancestors rhythm
rocking, homeward bound

Sunrise on the River

shy dawn tenderly,
gold tongue kisses the rippling
river's flowing face

Til Death Do Us Part

rain or shine each day
we celebrate a sacred
love affair with life

Secondline Send Off

here we raise the dead
hoist them heavenward on winged
music hades hot

Quarter Moon Rise

soft moon shimmers out
of cloudy dress, stirred by night's
suggestive caress

All Nite Long

amid dancing and
drinking til dewed dawn, nights stretch
24 hours long

The Spice of Life

cayenne in our blood
we dance, eat, laugh, cry & love
with peppered passion

Round Midnight, Place de Congo

through congoed leaves of
griot trees zephyred spirits
breathe unshackled dreams

Spiritual Geography

this crescent's arc is
africa, its bayoued blues
breath exhales blackness

St. Louis Cemetery Crypt

bones float in raised stone,
white, altared graves blood transformed
become black souled thrones

Makes You Go Oohhh!

sing of lusty foods
so savory they buck jump
cross your tongue's dance floor

Height, Breadth, Depth

tropic green days, red
erotic evenings, cultured
black nights: New Orleans

I Live in the Mouth of History

i live in the mouth of history
but wish that civilization would spit me out
modernity's split tongue lies, progress' white teeth bite
& the ancient seed of my blackness is never swallowed
though my weary bones are cracked and tender marrow sucked

i live in the belly of genocide
the acid of injustice daily eating away at my gentleness
separating me into useful proteins, vitamins & invaluable
human fibers which nourish the blood of a body which rejects
the bulk of my being & shits me out of the ass of a demented society
which self righteously accuses me of smelling up the place

i live in the heart of irrational jingoism
nitroglycerin in my brain & a pacemaker restraining my freedom
of movement, my every emotional impulse is suspect—the teachers
want to know why can't i reduce the butt of my desires
to a flat acceptance of infrequent love making

i live for the day when i can wake up
without voices of morality telling me to hate being who i am
without images of consumption suggesting the brightest life is white
without broadcasts of commercialism prostituting my womanself
without sirens of authority seeking to incarcerate black male genitalia
without bullets of unfriendly fire lacerating the social air

i live for the day when i can wake up
& see morning smiles blackening my mirror
& caress the intimate nudity of all whom i love

& inhale a bouquet of communal unity aromas
& hear a liturgy of love & respect chanted every hour
& taste tomorrow in all its bittersweet complexity

i live for that day & love the night
even as a prisoner in the skin of humanity
whether as ancestor, advocate or spirit unborn
i was, am and will continue to be
a dangerous rock in the mouth of this century's history

I Just Heard John Buffington Died

an incredibly bright blue almost white open sky
with distant puffs of slow moving cottony clouds
birds floating, brown kites with heart, feathers & song, it's
tom dent's birthday, he & i are sharing little moments like
i imagine bird & diz must have done off the stand,
maybe between sets or on a train, in a car, or just standing
on a corner, two creative, hip, sophisticated but unjaded
men savoring the spiritual charm of one love
tom tells me: john buffington died this day

driving back to my work space, negotiating the laughing colors
of big easy street life i spy young black new orleans women
beautiful as only they can be, walk-swaying through
this infant soft afternoon giving gleam to the sunshine,
a feminine kaleidoscope of skin color, hair texture, body build
& dimpled attitude, ah yes, this life can be mighty good

there is nothing sad about today, the pine tree in front
of my office porch is laughing, the weather is an afro-french kiss
every nuance encourages contentment & the giving of thanx
to be here & now witnessing the wonderfulness of these moments

& yet john buffington has died
life is like that
even when it's fucked up it's beautiful
especially when beautiful, something sad
is going down somewhere—still like an eternal faucet
for every painful hole that death leaves
some other great goodness flowingly fills the gap

on some less enjoyable day when everyone i know is well
i will think back to the bittersweet bliss i tasted
on the afternoon i heard my friend john buffington died
& ironically identify the euphoric radiance of this death day
as a wondrous transitional tribute the creator
gave to the generous spirit of john buffington

Always Know

and now i know
you intimately
touching your
emotional nudity
i hear your voice, familiar
as my own, sounding
iconoclastic chords
of closeness

in the seriousness
of this moment
our passion is
ironically serrated
by serene subtle silences
which reverberate stronger
than any words, much like
Monk masterly making
seminal statements
out of what he doesn't
play

if i didn't
care, i could come and go, run
the changes and split, but this
is real music
and so now even after
departing, our motions
have indelibly, albeit
invisibly, marked the interior
of our flesh, deep
wherein resides our realness

and like a song by Sphere
—whose music lives
surviving his passing—
beauty is a sacred seed
ever continuing in the host
of everyone it truly
touches

so even as our shining
moment of mutuality
slips softly into the air
swallowed by history,
having experienced
each other's
rhythms

we will
always know

"5 Minutes, Mr. Salaam"

some
times
i
get
so
lone
ly
for
u
i
feel
like
calling
up
the
devil
and
making
a
deal
—you

know
like
take
my
soul
i
just
want
her
to
hold
me
for
five
minutes

Sonia Sanchez

Sonia Sanchez, born in 1935, is the author of more than a dozen books, including Homecoming, We a BaddDDD People, homegirls & hand-grenades, and her most recent, Wounded in the House of a Friend. She has received an American Book Award and the Peace and Freedom Award from the Women's International League for Peace and Freedom. She is Laura Carnell Professor of English and Women's Studies at Temple University.

Poem for July 4, 1994
For President Václav Havel

1.

It is essential that Summer be grafted to
bones marrow earth clouds blood the
eyes of our ancestors.
It is essential to smell the beginning
words where Washington, Madison, Hamilton,
Adams, Jefferson assembled amid cries of:

> "The people lack information"
> "We grow more and more skeptical"
> "This Constitution is a triple-headed
>   monster"
> "Blacks are property"

It is essential to remember how cold the sun
how warm the snow snapping
around the ragged feet of soldiers and slaves.
It is essential to string the sky
with the saliva of Slavs and
Germans and Anglos and French
and Italians and Scandinavians,
and Spaniards and Mexicans and Poles
and Africans and Native Americans.
It is essential that we always repeat:
> we the people,
> we the people,
> we the people.

2.

"Let us go into the fields" one
brother told the other brother. And
the sound of exact death
raising tombs across the centuries.
Across the oceans. Across the land.

3.

It is essential that we finally understand:
this is the time for the creative
human being
the human being who decides
to walk upright in a human
fashion in order to save this
earth from extinction.

This is the time for the creative
Man. Woman. Who must decide
that She. He. Can live in peace.
Racial and sexual justice on
this earth.

This is the time for you and me.
African American. Whites. Latinos.
Gays. Asians. Jews. Native
Americans. Lesbians. Muslims.
All of us must finally bury
the elitism of race superiority
the elitism of sexual superiority
the elitism of economic superiority
the elitism of religious superiority.

So we welcome you on the celebration
of 218 years Philadelphia. America.

So we salute you and say:
Come, come, come, move out into this world
nourish your lives with a
spirituality that allows us to respect
each other's birth.
come, come, come, nourish the world where

every 3 days 120,000 children die
of starvation or the effects of starvation;
come, come, come, nourish the world
where we will no longer hear the
screams and cries of women, girls,
and children in Bosnia, El Salvador,
Rwanda . . . AhAhAhAh AHAHAHHHHH

>Ma-ma. Dada. Mamacita. Baba.
>Mama. Papa. Momma. Poppi.
>The soldiers are marching in the streets
>near the hospital but the nurses say
>we are safe and the soldiers are
>laughing marching firing calling
>out to us i don't want to die i
>am only 9 yrs old, i am only 10 yrs old
>i am only 11 yrs old and i cannot
>get out of the bed because they have cut
>off one of my legs and i hear the soldiers
>coming toward our rooms and i hear
>the screams and the children are
>running out of the room i can't get out
>of the bed i don't want to die Don't
>let me die Rwanda. America. United
>Nations. Don't let me die . . . .

And if we nourish ourselves, our communities
our countries and say
>no more hiroshima
>no more auschwitz
>no more wounded knee
>no more middle passage
>no more slavery
>no more Bosnia
>no more Rwanda

No more intoxicating ideas of
racial superiority
as we walk toward abundance
we will never forget

>the earth
>the sea

      the children
      the people

For *we the people* will always be arriving
a ceremony of thunder
waking up the earth
opening our eyes to human
monuments.
      And it'll get better
      it'll get better
if *we the people* work, organize, resist,
come together for peace, racial, social
and sexual justice
      it'll get better
      it'll get better.

This Is Not a Small Voice

This is not a small voice
you hear　　　　this is a large
voice coming out of these cities.
This is the voice of LaTanya.
Kadesha. Shaniqua. This
is the voice of Antoine.
Darryl.　　Shaquille.
Running over waters
navigating the hallways
of our schools spilling out
on the corners of our cities and
no epitaphs spill out of their river mouths.

This is not a small love
you hear　　　　this is a large
love, a passion for kissing learning
on its face.
This is a love that crowns the feet with hands
that nourishes, conceives, feels the water sails
mends the children,
folds them inside our history where they
toast more than the flesh
where they suck the bones of the alphabet
and spit out closed vowels.

This is a love colored with iron and lace.
This is a love initialed Black Genius.

This is not a small voice
you hear.

Saundra Sharp

Saundra Sharp, born in 1942, is a writer, producer, filmmaker, and actress. She has written four volumes of poetry, including Typing in the Dark *and* Soft Song. *She performs her work on stage in* On the Sharp Side, *also the title of her poetry album. Ms. Sharp is based in Los Angeles, where she is a volunteer literacy tutor and Black women's health advocate.*

Tribal Marks

She stopped traffic
crossing 6th and Berendo
    skirt too short
    yellow too loud
I saw her draped in the woven cloth of the Maasai
    feet too dirty
    blouse too tight
    titties too sharp
I saw Samburu hips arched in prayer as
her hands pulled milk from her favorite cattle
    hair too nappy
    skin blue black
she stood layered in bangles and necklaces
brushing a gnat from her unwavering eye
exposed bronze scalp holding a face bathed in ochre

    slothful, my mother would say
    slewfoot, my grandmother would notice
    Those Negroes, my aunt would remark,
    still carrying some of where they came from
    with them
as warm rift valley soil eased between her toes
Tribal marks.

In a gesture of declaration
claiming 6th and Berendo she
waved the blackened cloth across her butt
lifted one long unshaven arm in the air and
let the black float out the arch of her back

Tribal marks.

And where are mine?

Are they these
hips condensed into lycra girdles?
tongue fluent in symbols not my own?
feet stomping pavement I don't own?

Safe in our cars we waited unwillingly
as she
flaunted 6th St.
too tight and dirty
slewfoot and slothful
dancing grandly with
tribal marks
she can not recognize
while I grasped for remembrance,
wondering
where did I leave mine?

Good Nights

the earth moves
the sirens flare
a choir of car burglar alarms sings
om in six electronic keys
neighbors edge into the street
for the first time since . . .
the last time.
I sit on the broken step
release myself to the unquiet darkness
and bathe in the good nights.

> *"Oh Mary Mack, Mack, Mack*
> *All dressed in black, black, black*
> *With silver buttons, buttons, buttons*
> *All down her back, back, back. . . ."*

Cleveland nights
catching fireflies in Mason jars as
tenor crickets herald heat
another piece of Nana's lemon meringue pie
growing in a womb of all is well

"She asked her mother, mother, mother
For fifteen cents, cents, cents
To see the elephant, elephant, elephant
Jump the fence, fence, fence. . . ."

mesmerized by the talk of grown folks
please pretty please can I sleep
        on the porch tonight?
Good nights.

Camp nights
low coals and bronzed marshmallows
girl scout very american nights
bright girl voices
singing bonds, singing promises

"Follow, follow, follow the dream
Of young and old, of green and gold
Follow, follow, follow the dream. . . ."

firelight nights for dreamers
Good nights.

Addis Ababa nights
a taxi slips through the unstillness
racing against curfew
the melody of Ethiopia at the Hilton
still caressing my toes
I thank my driver for the Cinderella ride
say "Hello" in perfect Amharic
(I thought I said "good night." . . .)
Good nights.

"The neon lights are always bright on Broadway
Gonna be on Broadway, gonna be on Broadway,
Gonna be on Broadway, gonna be on Broadway. . . ."

Broadway nights
    the other Broadway
sidestepping police
their hips holding hands locked in prayer
around their penis clubs
congas riff off the roofs

proclaiming heat, sweat, territory
hot nights,
Good nights.

Harlem nights
the politically correct collect
at Kimako's
"Trying to make it real. . . .
compared to what? . . . ."
Preachrighton! is a revolutionary sweet
the poets on a sugar high
heady with comprehension
and hope
and information—
some secret is being born here
and we are all the designated godmother
with a Temptations sidestep
we move The Movement to
chicken & waffles at Wells'
the poets grease, and
(as we head back downtown)
mock the impatient dawn
with Smokey song
Good nights.

Ouagadougou nights
kicking red dust in the sweaty softness
attentive to the heave of sleeping camels
feeling the muted music of the balafon
hold me to sleep
Good nights.

Antigua nights
surrender my audience to slot machines
wild horses play nearby
watchful that I don't steal their berries
the laughter of the musicians bounces
off my back
as I lift my evening gown
to tease the Antiguan tide
singing nights
Good nights.

Surinam nights
toe dancing with the River that
splits the land
pulls it back together,
the River that holds the moon
the stars are warriors
telling me how they got ovah
We make a pact,
the Surinamese warriors and me
Good nights.

Ancestor nights
in the middle of Virginia's National Forest
the lovers dance with the ancestors
in celebration of having found each other
pretending it is Africa
pretending we are home
believing for a moment
that the actor in the white house
does not control this space
full moon love nights
Good nights.

Santa Ana nights
I whip barefoot like a kite
through the Pacific sand
singing my answers to the dark
A white dove swoops down from the South
drops the questions on
12 grains of sand
I thank Obatala.
This is a good night.

the earth moves
the firecrackers that mark
Satchmo's birthday
flare across
the stench of garbage
I sit on the broken step
release myself to the
whispering spirits
and bathe in the good nights.

> earthquake Los Angeles
> July 4th weekend

In the Tradition of Bobbitt

He raped
she wept
He hit
she healed
He slept
she cut
the core of his ego

He's pitied
she's feared
He's innocent
she's insane
He's free
she's blamed—
for meditating first

Clergy despaired
comics screamed
plastic surgeons dreamed
But on Wall St.
silent women
sent the stock in butcher knives
up 14 percent.

Patricia Smith

Patricia Smith, born in 1955, is the author of Life According to Motown, Big Towns, Big Talk, which won the 1993 Carl Sandburg Award, and Close to Death. She has performed widely and is four-time individual champion of the National Poetry Slam. A columnist for the Boston Globe, Smith also worked for the Chicago Sun-Times as an arts critic.

Building Nicole's Mama

For the 6th grade class of Lillie C. Evans School, Liberty City, Miami

I am astounded at their mouthful names—
Lakinishia, Fumilayo, Chevellanie, Delayo—
their ragged rebellions and lipglossed pouts,
and all those pants drooped as drapery.
I rejoice when they kiss my face, whisper wet
and urgent in my ear, make me their obsession
because I have brought them poetry.
They shout raw, bruise my wrists with pulling
and brashly claim me as mama as they rip me
from the cross and cradle my head in their little laps
waiting for new words to grow in my mouth.

You. You. *You.*
Angry, jubiliant, weeping poets—we are all
saviors, reluctant Jesuses in the limelight,
but you knew that, didn't you? Then let us
bless this sixth grade class, 40 nappy heads,
40 cracking voices, and all of them
raise their hands when I ask. They have all seen
the Reaper, grim in his heavy robe,
pushing the button for the dead project elevator,
begging for a break at the corner pawn shop,
cackling wildly in the back pew of the Baptist church.

I ask the death question and brown fists
punch the air, *me!*, *me!*, and O'Neal,
matchstick crack child, watched his mother's
body become a claw and 9-year-old Tiko Jefferson,
barely big enough to lift the gun, fired a bullet
into his own throat after mama bended his back

211

with a lead pipe. Tamika cried into a sofa pillow
when daddy blasted mama into the north wall
of their cluttered one-room apartment,
Donya's cousin gone in a driveby, dark window,
click, click, gone, says Donya, her tiny finger
a barrel, the thumb a hammer. I am astonished
at their losses—and yet when I read a poem
about my own hard-eyed teenager, Jeffery asks
He is dead yet?

It cannot be comprehended,
my 18-year-old still pushing and pulling
his own breath. And 40 faces pity me,
knowing that I will soon be as they are,
numb to our bloodied histories,
favoring the Reaper with a thumbs up and a wink,
hearing the question and screeching *me, me,
Miss Smith, I know somebody dead!*

Can poetry hurt us? they ask me before
snuggling inside my words to sleep. *I love you,*
Nicole says, Nicole wearing my face,
pimples peppering her nose, and she is as black
as angels are. Nicole's braids clipped, their ends
kissed with match flame to seal them, and *can you
teach me to write a poem about my mother?
I mean, you write about your daddy and he dead,
can you teach me to remember my mama?*
A teacher tells me this is the first time Nicole
has admitted that her mother is gone,
murdered by slim silver needles and a stranger
rifling through her blood, the virus pushing
her skeleton through for Nicole to see.
And now this child with rusty knees and
mismatched shoes sees poetry as her scream
and asks me for the words to build her mother
again, replacing the voice, stitching on the lost flesh.

So poets,
as we take the stage,
as we
flirt and sin and rejoice behind microphones—
remember Nicole.

She knows that we are here now,
and she is an empty vessel waiting to be filled.

And she is waiting.

And she is waiting.

And she waits.

Finding His Fist
Interviewing Nelson Mandela

I want to scream into the pink hearing aid nestled in his hairy ear, *Where is your fist?* Thick-throated men in black coats scurry to the windows of the suite, scour the landscape with slitted eyes, approximate the arc of bullets. They move me from one chair to another to another until I am sitting so close to him his breath sparks moisture on my skin. The pink contraption, imitating another flesh, fills his ear and again I want to howl, to startle, to prickle his nose hairs, but then I notice that he is not the vapor I imagined. I thought his body would be a temporary thing with fingers, an ear, an arm misting into nothing at odd intervals, features folding into dust, all symptoms of the recently caged. He smoothes a wrinkle in his gray suit, grins sheepishly, leans forward waiting for a question. I stare at his fist resting on the polished table. I scream with my mouth closed. He hears me perfectly.

Meanwhile, In Rwanda

There is a freedom too, a peculiar kind,
a freedom forged of dust and blade
and the stretched swoon of a mother
who cannot lift her hand to reach her child,
who cannot lift his head to see his mother.
In Johannesburg, the flags snap in fall air.
The new president giggles and dances backwards.
White women sip champagne with their maids
and posters of the losers blaze on the boulevard.
In my hotel room, I press my fingers
against the television screen, harder, harder,
hoping to break through
and flick the flies from the child's cheek,

pry open the sealing eyes.
No, I want to use those fingers to stop my ears,
to block out the doomed screeches
as wail-eyed warriors move from house to house,
killing the windows, stabbing the floors,
stinging the roof with bullets, driving a scythe
through a family's sinew. The river swells with bodies,
bloated bumper cars careening in the stinking surf.
His voice tinny from Boston, my editor calls
and says they talked about sending me over,
since I was already *so close.*

I leave the television on, craving voices.
The camera lingers as a tiny soul slips
from the child's bony body and waves goodbye.

The Woman Who Died In Line
Election Day, Soweto

Let us call her footnote, oddity, heart tug,
anecdote. For music, name her Tashi.
To enliven the telling, say she wavered,
almost imperceptibly, on thick-soled sandals
and that gray skin thickened her heels.
Was she humming? Imagine a vibing wire
running through the center of her body
as a bowl of history teetered on her head,
an offering balanced between those two
fat, beautiful and nappy braids of silver.
A copper bracelet, rumored to heal, purify
and protect, bit into her old wrist. She believed it.
Let's call her irony, bad joke, God's idle comeuppance.
For the sake of rhythm, we'll name her Mary.

Perhaps the land shifted slightly to receive her,
mother of tortured breathing and thin hips,
sister believing in red headwrap, the tossing of bones,
copper wire burning one old wrist,
Tashi for the sake of music,
and no one to translate her gorgeous sigh
or to prepare the cool dust for her weight.
One moment she tall, wire hum,

breast and belly warm beneath raw cotton.
And then, to enliven the telling,
let's say that we all saw her die,
that we dangled freedom before her thin-hipped angel,
and that the angel laughed, and told us the woman's real name.

Christopher Stanard

Christopher Stanard was born in Washington, D. C., in 1967 and raised in Charlotte, North Carolina. A graduate of Morehouse and Georgia Tech, Stanard's poetry has appeared in several publications, including Catalyst *and* Drumvoices Revue.

Baseball

Granddaughters' bright smiles, chili dogs, and lemonade in the shade start old men to
    reminiscing,
Just like Little League games played on sultry summer Saturdays in Summerhill or
    Southwest Atlanta.
A pair of wizened octogenarians, 86 and 88, sit silently in the stands,
    smiling just because
It feels so good to be right here, right now, wearing Atlanta Braves hats;
It feels so very good to see their little brown boys step up to the plate and
    swing their bats.
It feels so good, yet it hurts enough to cry . . .
Thinking about the old days, the ABCs of the old Negro League—
The Atlanta Black Crackers, Birmingham Black Barons, Josh Gibson, Cool Papa Bell,
    Satchel Paige,
And all those other greats who swung majestic bats with mighty hearts,
    major league talent,
But received only minor respect in their day—footnotes today, but not
    forgotten.
The older man adjusts his cap, casually wipes away a lone tear, and smiles.
David Justice turns at him and winks as he signs autographs for all the
    kids.

Rap Is

Rap is no mystery.
It's simply straight and pure history
broken down into knowledge pieces and bits/hits in a pot
sprinkled with the force of Salt 'N Peppa on top

hip-hop spiced and spliced with reggae, base-ill, and be-bop
straight up from the soul of 125th Street, righteously.
Like the force of a fist, rap is raw reality,
attitude with flavor, anecdotes to savor, for real.
It's something you've just gotta sample and feel.

Still, rap is more than just a sample on the strength.
It's a voice that cannot be silenced;
a raging fire that cannot be quenched;
a roaring spirit that lives forever large in living color
worldwide hard-core, sister to brother.

Rap is New Jack Swing like Teddy, but I don't mean to deceive;
it's a Flash of Old School Cool like Starsky, you gotta believe.
Rap is powerful poetry mcs recite
while movin' the crowd in the middle of the night.
Is it fake gangsters talkin' trash? Yeah, right. Psyche!
Rap is no joke, but when all is said and done,
rap is music De La Soul; rap is not a gun.

It's Assata's song, one love, a children's story, a message to everyday
      people in
Tennessee.
It's Roxanne, Roxanne, and all her MCI friends and family,
sometimes even Bobby Jimmy & the Critters and 20 answer records with
      a dis from AT&T.
It's 20 kilos of Miami base thumpin' your paint job off;
glass-shakin', invigorating, it could never be soft.

Rap is the wisdom of the griot with the sound of the drum;
it's roots extended deep to where you come from.
It's a call for respect and a quest for knowledge;
it's the Leaders of the New School to the Boyz in College.

Rap is for winners, merciless to beginners, no suckers allowed.
Step off the stage if the crowd doesn't/don't go wild.
Stay on if it does and deliver knowledge strong
until the break
until the break
until the break of day
until the break of dawn.

Washington Square Park and a Game of Chess

One, two, three,
four tiny black wheels on a Dove Bar Cart
thump bumpity-bump
bumpity-bump, bumpity-bump
over little round pebbles
and dark blue asphalt.
Like a Good Humor Truck
sans motor, sans music,
but still happily filled
with ice cream,
the tiny tumbrel rolls along,
pushed by the hands
of a blue-capped brown boy
in new acid-washed
blue-jean overalls
and a red/white striped shirt.
Drawing attention like a brush
in a cubist's dream,
it thumps along under the cedar shade
on the canvas of
Washington Square Park.
Bumpity-bump mixes with the sounds
of blue jays singing,
boom boxes blasting,
and a pink freckle-faced girl pleading
"Daddy! Daddy! Ice cream! Ice cream!"
as she points to the spot
where both a Japanese beetle
and a buzzing bumblebee converge
hoping for a bumpity-bump sweet
vanilla ice cream/chocolate treat.

A web is cast as the cart
bumpity-bumps on by
an old Rastafarian, who looks up
from his game of chess,
his concentration captured
by the passing sound
and his emotions enticed
by the thought of a soft summer breeze
and a Dove Bar in the shade . . .

but the cart rolls away,
its bumpity-bump refrain fading
like the gray wisps of smoke
from his pipe.
With a sigh,
the old man straightens his back
and surveys the scene
on the chessboard before him.
His brow furrows,
his dark eyes stare intently,
and his lips purse,
puffing hard on his pipe.
The old general
ponders his move,
waiting, debating, hesitating
until
a decision is made,
a gambit is played,
and the battle is rejoined
with loud clicks
arhythmically sounded out by
hands slamming down hard
on a Janus-faced clock
sentry standing just left
of fallen black and white knights,
testimonies to the
fierceness of the fray.
Two impetuous pawns
meet their fates, sacrificed
as a third scales a castle
and threatens the adversary's king.
The king flees, but to no avail;
The Rasta's bishop spirits through the air
to settle on the queen's square.
Her king kneels to his fate
and resigns.
The battle is done;
the war is ended.

The victorious Rasta rises, laughs,
turns to leave, and ambles off
down the path
where children climb monkey bars

with hands sticky
from vanilla ice cream/chocolate
to catch the receding sound
of bumpity-bump,
bumpity-bump,
bumpity.

Wrong Color

Gray suit.
Blue day.
Great telephone interview.
They say they like my resumé.
But
When the interviewer sees me
He does a double take.
Damn.
I knew I should have worn the blue suit.

lamont b. steptoe

lamont b. steptoe was born in 1949 and reared in Pittsburgh, Pennsylvania. He is the author of six books of poetry: Crimson River, American Morning/Mourning, Catfish and Neckbone Jazz, Mad Minute, Uncle Sam's South China Sea Blue Nightmare, *and* Dusty Road.

Window Shopping

us po' Black boys
walked the streets of the 1950's
Pittsburgh business district
on Sundays
dazzled by the attire
of the white dummies
in the department store windows
the "Stacy Adams" shoes
the "Brooks Brothers" suits
the "Stetson" hats
belonged on "our" bodies
those silk ascots
those gold cuff links
would be ours
if we could but sell enough papers
hock enough "pop" bottles
run enough errands
beg and borrow long enough
With those shoes, those suits
those fine button downed shirts
would come beautiful women and love
and sports cars
and a house on a hill overlooking the sea
and wonderful kids
and everything glorious
just like in the movies
and we would forget
our dark painful roots
mired in poverty and racism
in a steel town
that used "niggers" like "iron ore"
in the blast furnace of life

Sweet Brown Rice and Red Bones

the sun
bronzes your browns
reddens your yellows
honeys your skin
it is 1994
and ten years later
your beauty
still conquers me
turns me into
a black panther
blinded by the instinct
of mating
some old flame
is still dining on the oxygen
of desire
once again
i want to lose myself
in your jungle
become entranced
by a thousand jabbering monkeys
drunk on a million starry nights
i'm remembering our time
that was all heat
and man/woman scent
peppered with sherry and smoke
i'm remembering
how deep i traveled
into your forest
how hard i worked
to drown
in your rivers
how long it took
to gather the fragments
after the explosion
i'm remembering
how good the good times were
the hot summer nights
on the stoop with lightning bugs
our most "intimate witnesses"
the discussions

that covered everything
from hell to heaven
the sweet brown rice of our love
that was once a rainbow
arching over our dreams

Notes for a Poem from the Middle Passage of Years

when
they speak of my death
tell them that it was the lack of love
that killed me

tell them
it was betrayal
of family, friends
and country that killed me

tell them
it was a delayed fuse
an unexploded mine
from the Vietnam war
that killed me

tell them
it was the unpaid debts
of Native American genocide
and the African Holocaust

tell them
it was how they wounded each other
how they
destroyed their children
how they destroyed themselves
how they destroyed faith
in God
LOVE and PEACE

tell them
it was the incessant barrage
of suffering

that wounded my eyes
my heart
my spirit
from the nightly news
that killed me

tell them
it was the horror
the unspeakable horror
of Haiti
Rwanda
Liberia
Somalia
Bosnia-Herzegovina
Gaza
South Africa
the streets of America
that slew me

tell them
it was the things
so-called friends whispered
mumbled
rumored

tell them
it was witnessing
the less bright
the less talented
the less principled
get ahead
make millions
while
the bright and principled
the talented and truthtellers
the dreamers
were slain or starved
jailed or exiled
or forgotten

tell them
that it was how they wounded
the land for greed

how they raped
poisoned and shattered
the earth

tell them
it was the dread
of how all this must end
the dread of how soon
it will all be stopped
the dread
of how harsh
how severe
how awesome
how final
how unabetted the punishment
for this out-of-control
mechanical-computeristic phenomena
of intellect gone mad
with the dementia of titanic ego
will be . . .

tell them
that that's what killed me
that that is what exploded
in the palace
of the heart . . .

Mississippi Blues

I've
seen the Mississippi River
flowin' all big and wide
musclin' down the continent
blues all in its stride
I say
I've seen
the Mississippi River
flowin' all big and wide
musclin' down the continent
blues all in its stride
Bustin' out at "Nawlins"
headed for the wide, wide, sea

Bustin' out at "Nawlins"
headed for the wide, wide, sea
back to Africa baby
with a blue song from me
back to Africa baby
with a blue song from me

Sekou Sundiata

Sekou Sundiata is professor of writing at Eugene Long College in New York City. He was featured in the Bill Moyers PBS series on poetry, The Language of Life, *and his work appears in the anthology based on the series. A Sundance Film Institute Fellow and a former Charles H. Revson Fellow, Sundiata is currently producing his own poetry and music CD for Mouth Almighty/Mercury Records.*

Notes from the Defense of Colin Ferguson

In December of 1993, Colin Ferguson massacred 6 people and wounded 19 others on board an eastbound Long Island Railroad train. Claiming innocence, Ferguson acted as his own lawyer. He rejected the advice of his cocounsel who urged him to plead guilty by reason of insanity or guilty by reason of black rage.

The Time Leading Up To

Rush hour. I board the train
at Pennsylvania Station,
take a seat slip into my public solitude.

The steady racket of the wheels tracking
over the rails rocked me to sleep.

Then somebody went into my bag, took my piece
and unleashed. In the last days of 1993,

there were 93 charges filed against me.
My first clue that the count was off:
only 6 dead, only 19 wounded.

The Week in Review

The day I was sentenced to the rest of my life,
four people shot to death at a post office
in New Jersey. Last Sunday

Michael Jordan returned to the Bulls.
The newpaper said *the horizons brightened
immensely.* Not far from the basketball court

227

where the hero first returned,
yesterday Iron Mike Tyson stepped out
a free man. It's a wonder

the police didn't beat me more than they did.

The Case Through the Looking Glass

The shooter in Jersey, black. Air Jordan, black.
Iron Mike, black men like me.

93 into 93 is 12 which is 3 which is
the kind of mathematics we're dealing with.
Bad luck? Coincidence?

I'll never plead down to a black rage defense.
Privilege, position, previous condition
of servitude have nothing to do with it.

My lawyer said the People versus Me could be
a landmark. The New York Times called it
notorious, changing our view of the law.

If it's race at all it's Race with a big R,
the way you might call a lion a cat.
We are climbing abstraction's ladder,

every motion goes higher, higher: a black
into a man into certain people who at certain
times penetrate, breakthrough, destroy, create.

To Emerge from the Shadows

According to reports, I entered the third car
walked backwards down the aisle, looking
them in the eyes as I shot

one after the other. Several of the relatives
spoke. I took notes: *I will give you no hatred.
You are not worthy of my thought.*

Your justice is being served. I showed little
emotion, when they introduced the murder weapon,

the prosecution examined it, passed it
among themselves.

I asked for permission to hold it,
just to get the feel.

How many 9 mms. did they make
the year they made mine? It's the only way,
Your Honor, if you can imagine it,
it belongs to you.

When he said No, the trial was over.
Justice is for the guilty and the innocent.
I am neither one. So what was the point of going on

about the gun? They say I emptied it,
reloaded, began shooting again. I did not
utter a word. I believe

there is some privacy due to the victims,
even in death.

That Picture in the Paper

I come down too hard on myself sometimes.
Relax, I tell myself, be free, you did not come,
you were sent. Like a hurricane.

The ones people never forget, showing off
the knarled, broken trees, the bent submission
of survivors, makeshift memorials to the dead.

That picture in the paper mistook adrenaline
for violence in my eyes. Doe eyes, really.
They exaggerate under pressure.

Ask any deer crossing the road.

The Defense Rests

I used to sign my name with a flourish. No more
of that shit.
I want to be like a curtain raised,
now that I know the value

of a few words with power: 15 bullets,
15 dead and 20 wounded.
The count should have been just that
righteous. Then you could see

I was but the shadow, not the deed.
When you hear my name, what can you say
about yourself,

I never let the killer out, proud to say,
he's still right here with me?

Do angels keep falling?
Did Oedipus have a choice?
Why does the brutal father repeat
himself in the son?

Why do millions of Uncle Toms
each morning rise, hungry, thirsty,
sleep encrusted in their eyes?
Who knows why the crazy aunt goes crazy
at the family reunion?

What about Nat Turner? What about Stagolee?
Are they the same by other names?

I am where I stand, in a long line of myth:
Bigger Thomas, Charles Manson and the rest
walking down some street in Times Square,

born, like me, into a form. Some follow it,
some don't. People get ghosts they never asked for,
some long ago, exiled hurt mapping its way home.

Open Heart

Visiting hours are over.
You walk in, heart open

yet blocked by the non-stop
repeal of membrane
after membrane

to the cells
the count peeling back
the viscera
the bone the cartilage.

Here comes the Equinox,
fading daylight
balancing night, the world

seems in remission.
Its angles and edges flat
as the horizon.
On one side,

the unshakable absences.
On the other,
more of the past
than you care to love.

Some days you forget
where you parked the car,
you can't find

your house keys.
Finally you come
to believe in loss,

as a way of knowing
going down,

the body follows
its own intelligence,

it initiates
each outing in darkness.

The text for today
is early Miles,
the Columbia years.

That tone.
Pared down to essentials.
A bittersweet subtext

    of solids fluids
    and air

    somewhere
    between taps
    and reveille

Ear Training
For Fatisha

When in the empty city a siren blasts through the stop-go then gone the city empty returns to humming just below middle-c an unsettled heart maybe next door the heavy footed neighbor up at all hours shuffling across the floor in contrary motion the light coming through the window the color of Saturday with Sunday's face makes a pattern on the wall & the bedroom itself becomes something else like Art & Meaning meaning Coltrane playing ballads on the radio changes the whole house from a house to a space shrinking molecule by molecule your rolling rock your rivers to cross your daily Babel bouncing off the satellite bounces the earth into a world a unified theory of noise between the ears reflecting noise between the spheres sometimes drunk & singing out of tune tuned to the history of History & its estimated time of arrival at the cross worlds where what you do with the left hand can be a different matter from what you do with the right hand to integrate today yesterday distilled into a few mental arithmetics a few selected pages pages recollected under constant revision the relentless decision-making the past the Past with corrections erasures lines through circles in red playing off each other variations on a theme a theme of sums & totals & extended compositions all about Time as in sometimes you make it swing which means that Time probably always swings sometimes it swings only unto you like the wings of your personal angels fluttering a trill or two a cluster of triplets feather light signifying sources beyond the contours of the normal the regular the predictable you think about somebody & the telephone rings the wrong number a familiar voice nevertheless on the other end it seems like your name is being called an interior invitation a calling the way the sun often segues slowly into twilight pulling your breath out of your voice as if the conductor raised the baton & the chord you sang was awe

Making Poems
on the road in Minneapolis

We sit beside the Mississippi,
and Rhodessa says
there's a harvest of clouds
passing by. A black brown boy
pantomimes in time
to some private beat
only he can hear bouncing
around us and away.
Stephanie says
this is probably a sacred space
and he's feeling it in his head,
and boom! just like that,
he's feeling it in his head.

The same clouds you see
right here in Minneapolis
you see in Brooklyn
says Craig.
I'm from Brooklyn
says Rome.
and I never saw
those clouds
before in my life. It's the First

Annual Caribbean Festival,
and the mid-West Indians do
what they can
to conjure home,
but the jerk chicken
runs out quick,
the peas and rice is scarce,
and this close
to the Canadian border
the Americans outnumber
them 5 to 1.
When the deejay pumps
the rhythms,
what's missing has a voice
big as what's there,
so they navigate

the difference by heart,
from memory,
and the life of the moment as-is.
And doesn't this constitute
home, afterall?
This navigation, this location,
this building wherever
you are from the inside out?
This is where the poems I love
come from: home
and made from scratch.

We step carnival style
all the way
to the parking lot,
and Idris takes a snapshot:
one for the ready,
two for the show.
The camera blinks
and we blink back.
We don't even fix up
for the lens or smile
to pretend, pleased to be
composed among things
that belong together.
A river this big
must turn to the sea.
The same freeway come, go.
One sky covers all.

I've been troubled
for weeks how to teach
making poems,
and when the shutter
clicks it triggers
my syllabus to begin:
Half the time,
I don't know what to do next.
With each cloud, an image.
With each image, a window,
a frame, a feeling to conjugate,
words to be made to speak.
When things be rocking, I try to rock.

When they shake,
I shake by the grace
of days like this:
a general flowing
of endorphins swimming
from head to toe,
a chain of being
endlessly linking
cool to cool to cool.

Dorothy Perry Thompson

Dorothy Perry Thompson, born in 1944, is an associate professor at Winthrop University, where she teaches poetry writing, American literature, African American Studies, and composition. A member of the Board of Governors of the South Carolina Academy of Authors, her poems have appeared in Caesura, Crucible, Catalyst, African American Review, Sucarnoochee Review, and Carolina Literary Companion. Her first book of poetry, Fly with the Puffin, was published in 1995.

Intelligence Quotients
For Wally

Some of us know
porcelain, quiet
on glass-top tables,
lavender, and princess telephones,

wishing wells, piano lessons
and tennis bracelets
for Christmas.

Some of us know
roll-a-way beds
and army surplus blankets,
fatback and biscuit snacks,

creolin, drying
in the untreated wood
of a just-mopped floor,
a cold water flat's
best sanitizer.

Some of us know
mahogany railings, white gloves,
scallops for supper,
and how to get Daddy at the office.

Some of us know
the yellow skin of chicken feet
boiling gray in onions and water,

six small tin plates waiting
for them every Monday night.

Some of us play
word games in the den
and get stock statements
in the mail.

Some of us pack
the necessary lunch
for waiting in the free clinic line,
and sigh the relief
of brand new paint spots
on Daddy's work boots.

Dancing in Menopause

Instead of icepacks
pressed against my forehead
for more than a week
(they make dark blotches
on my skin)

I'd rather have a pretty boy, hip-singing
gliding in black (silk shirt
and front-pleated baggy slacks),
showing off on the dance floor
just for me, then cautiously
braving his way to my table
just to say hello. If he says
he likes my yellow dress, I let him
smile at the drape of it over
my brown thigh.

We will not touch.
It is enough to spread our arms
and hover, eye to eye,
not caring who leaves first,
which one watches the other
arcing toward another
pattern of flight.

Laurel Street, 1950

For Lottie Ashford Thompson

Big yellow woman
with careful fingers
made newspaper kites
and raced under them
with him
in the field
at the bottom of the hill.

They run out straight, fast,
watching the black and white shapes
gather air. Suddenly, she turns,
making her kite do smart, sharp dips.
She shows the boy how to let out
the string
'til he can no longer see
the stretched backbone,
the cross she tied to a picture
of Eisenhower's face.

When they reach the good,
dizzy place,
she falls, laughing
in the grass.

It was the time
when he could stumble
down the hall,
wipe sleep from
his eyes and see her
in the rocker,
baby brother Larry
pulling breakfast
from her perfect mound
of yellow flesh.

There were also
homemade slingshots, bows
and arrows made with sticks
and Coca-Cola bottle tops,

before Larry's two-year-old
heart failed
in the woodpile
at the back of the house,

before Slum-gullion,
her throw-in-anything,
I'm-sick-and-tired soup,
before her trips with Mae
to The Elbow Room,
her little brown bags
behind the bed.

Now,
the boy stands in the kitchen,
graying into 40,
folding
big red Circuit City ads:
bottom corners up, top corner down,
shaky fingers shaping
rough paper dragons.

Blues at 1

Koko Taylor sang
We gon' pitch a wang dang doodle
all night long,
shook her fist
and admonished listeners to tell
such folk as Pistol Packin' Sam,
Automic Jim and others about the Doodle.

She sweated purple
from eye shadow, streams also
going from a jheri-curled wig down
to creases in her ample neck, shoulders,
and arms.

                    The blue quiana
dress sparkled in front, rhinestoned.
Thin fabric stretched across the left shoulder

but swooped low below the other, just covering
the top of her right breast.

Above the elbow of thick right
forearm, a deep depression, too big
to be a dimple: her body's way
of remembering the bullet, the gun
held by a too shaky hand,
a too drunk man
trying to love her to death.

All night long, all night long,
she wailed, leaning back, opening
her mouth wide, showing dark
gaps between protruding teeth.
Red eyes, raspy voice, close-mouthed
pout ended each rhythmic phrase,
daring anybody to doubt
that wherever Koko and the Wang Dang
happen on Saturday night
is the place
to be.

Sister Lakin and Lally

Sister Lakin and Lally
usually came out together—
to go to the store,
to get a drink
or pay a debt.

Sister was a "high yaller"
slew-footed woman, tall and thin,
a fortyish good looking
like a partially used up
Cotton Club beauty.

Lally was darker,
with sagging cheeks
and deep frown lines.
She sometimes looked
like a sad bulldog—

water in her eyes,
but glad to have
a proud, high-steppin master
to lead her around.
    She went, or stayed
wherever Sister pointed
and was usually ready
to place a cigarette
between her friend's lean
and confident fingers.

In the beginning
Sister's looks
had got her Slick Jack
the smiling money man.
For a few years
she drove around proud
in a yellow Thunderbird
with white racing stripes.

Then the two babies,
Fred and Jack Jr.,
made her change.
    While Slick was busy
wheeling and dealing,
Sister found booze
and Lally Moore.

A little brown woman, Lally
looked like a tired Nina Simone blues:
    Go 'way from me everybody
    'cause I'm in my sin.
    Go 'way from me everybody,
    'cause I'm in my sin.
    Just fill me full of good liquor—
    somebody give me my gin.

Lally seemed strong only
when Sister got drunk.
She'd stand her up straight
and guide her through the alley
from the liquor house
home to the boys.

For years they walked
one beside the other,
Sister the proud stallion
pushing her knees
outward and against
the fabric of her narrow
tight-fitting skirts,
Lally silent, moving below her,
the Pall Malls sticking
from her front coat pocket.

Askia M. Touré

Askia M. Touré, born in 1938, is author of Juju, Songhai!, *and* From the Pyramids to the Projects, *for which he received an American Book Award in 1989. He is published in Paris, Rome, India, and China as well. A poetry volume,* Dawn Song! *is due in 1996. Touré works and resides in Atlanta, Georgia.*

Azuri

For Oaré

Azure, essence of change and horizons,
the wind whispering mortality across
bronze fortresses
    of the will. The sea, that
    womb-like symbol, singing
    our fetal beginnings.

Blue haze of dusk, the clear rain
beading your face and hair
as you wander,
    lost in ecstatic complexities of love.
    My solo soars among blind faces:
    a prodigal sojourn implying
    foghorn serenades in misty harbors,
    conjuring ghost ships voyaging
    through memory's night.

Somewhere, beyond
conventional categories,
    you wait. Your entrance
a phoenix-song glorifying
a catalytic future. The planes
of your face obscured by
the arrogant wind raging across
endless horizons, westwards,
to haunt an innocent calm.
I move with the familiar
    shuffle of a blind beggar;
searching always for the door

that opens perpetually upon
eternal summer. The years
have forged an azure luminance
to existence;

My reverie has been to recapture that ageless
    splendor embodied in your touch.
Blue shadows of dreams, echoes
    of turquoise emotions
    haunting turbid
    immensities impeding
    my rush through violent years.
Always, along the icy rivers flowing
    towards barbarous vistas,
    I have championed the consummate
    sweetness you radiate
    when your sunny tenderness
    ripens the fruits of desire.

Blue rattle of death down mythical corridors:
    the echoes of necessity
    looming like pharoanic colossi
    in moonlit temples of lost magnificence.
The galaxy surging with symphonic radiance,
    dwarfing my finite despair.
    I challenge eternity with Osirian
    arrogance: its lofty ignorance
    suffers in the absence of your shadow.
    Summits of Kilimanjaro are foothills
    lost in the passion of your eyes.

Somewhere, in a landscape lush with
    voluptuous summer, our paths will cross.
    My solo will be vibrant, though my
    instrument be tarnished and scarred.
My eyes will blossom seeing you gather
    serenity like your kente loppa
    gathers a palette of the sun.
    Till then, I wander the centuries—from
    indigo epochs through sapphire ages—
    guarding my tenderness like
    the rarest treasures of earth.

Blue scars on the soul:
> the heart pumping traumas that fester
> and bleed wild poetrys illuminating
> the visage of death.

The sunbird spreads its golden wings
> across valleys of forever,
> while my guitar laughs with the red
> voice of autumn's wild rain.

The harvests of tears are seething
> with random hungers
> exacerbating the madness in men,
> lashing them from bleak hovels to
> concrete tombs howling through
> nuclear nights.

Blue flames in the mind:
> a roaring defiance of "reality,"
> casting us as pariahs inhabiting shadowy
> sewers beneath the tread of aryan gods.

In the mornings of my song, I see your face
> aglow in sun-streaked gardens,
> amid the cries and chatter of songbirds:
> Black children leaping like gazelles:
> souls aflame with riotous being.

You are my rhapsody mellowing like vintage wine
> in the heart's hidden sanctuary. You are
> the song replacing fallen Pyramids,
> lost sagas captured in Coltrane solos,
> echoing Sudanic nobility.

Oaré, Oaré!
> take this blue zephyr, this errant shout,
> this passionate outburst from wild
> savannahs of midnight, into
> the healing waters of your dawn.

May the Lotus of your terra cotta loveliness
> nurture this lament, guard it
> till it grows into an oracle,
> a prophecy for apocalyptic jubilees
> in the anguished heart of Malcolm's sons.

O Lord of Light! A Mystic Sage
Returns to Realms of Eternity
For Master Sun Ra/ Sonny Blount
May 22, 1914–May 30, 1993

I.

He is sun-bright myth and Cosmic Light,
the audaciousness of comets sweeping through the inky abyss
of night,
the Solar Lord as pharoah of magic, mega-sounds, harmonious
with spectacular delights and unbridled flights aboard
the Melanin rocketship bound for the funk planets.
Ja man of Jupiterian wisdom, crowned prince of immortal night:
Lord Sun-Ra renamed,
renowned, resplendent in sparkling, sequined satins;
solar disc ablaze like a living Uraeus,[1] working his aural magic
among the tropic myths of reborn Kamites.[2] In the kingdoms
of his liberated soul, in realms of resurgent Negritude, we
celebrate his audacity, his expanded vision of
Possibility; moving beyond plastic parameters
of Anglo blandness, into multidimensional
space-time continuums,
restoring the broad-ranged, epic Consciousness of Cosmic Music,
embodied in a galaxy of master compositions, Alchemical
solos featuring Coltrane and Pharoah,
Don and Albert Ayler, Ornette Coleman, Sunny Murray, Milford Graves,
Marion Brown and myriad masters embracing
sacred pillars of the Sky Lords, Immortal Mansions of Ra.[3]

II.

He has moved beyond us, riding Shango's[4] lightning into stellar
parameters; a Moon Lord, changing his coat

1. A representation of the sacred asp on the headdress of Kemetic (Egyptian) rulers, symbolizing sovereignty.
2. From Kamit or Kemet (meaning the Black Land). The Kamites were the black people of the Black Land.
3. Ancient Kemetic (Egyptian) for Almighty God, Whose sacred symbol was the sun, as the Light of the Universe.
4. West Afrikan. Yoruba orisha symbolizing kingship, whose sacred presence was embodied in thunder and lightning bolts.

arrayed in cosmic colors; hanging with Tehuti,[5] embracing azure robes
of Isis,[6] soloing with Bird Diz Miles among expanses of inter-galactic
space ways, riding bursts of super-novas
brighter than a million mushroom bombs. A living Ancestor now
with Larry Neal, Henry Dumas[7]
legendary visionaries embodying all of our
sterling strengths, imaginative flights, volcanic passion, spanning
generations of Captivity and Resistance, deep pain
wild joy—the Cosmic Lord resplendent among us;
solar obelisk[8] of myth, long-breath solo of God-voice surging in
symphonies of light, phoenix flight of bright Bennu,[9] delighting
myriad choruses of angels, Orishas,[10] who
dance upon sun beams of his extended solos: O Lord of Light,
O Sun Prince transporting our tropic memories to emerald
mountains rising above primordial jungle dawns;
O Sky Lord roaring a Horus mantra in a dark abyss of Caucasian-
Neanderthal hell;
O Father, Osirian mage waving your pharoanic baton above choruses of
saxophones, possees of trumpets, bevies of thundering Afrikan drums
shaking the earth like Zulu legions.

III.

We mourn you when Whirlwinds roar and embrace our Marcus Garvey
rhapsodies above Middle Passage moans;
We mourn you when Midnight glides into our Consciousness wearing
a white gardenia above her
Billie Holiday face; when Sassy Vaughn launches her indigo-velvet
voice upon the mantras of our ecstasies.
We sing you, Father Ra-Osiris, asking that our memories continue
in your voyages to farthest reaches of the Universe, that they

5. Thoth, Greek. The Kemetic neter who symbolized knowledge, ancient wisdom, mystery, measurement of the heavens, phases of the moon.
6. Greek for Auset. The Nile Valley Civilization's Great Mother, "Queen of Heaven," "Throne of Kemet," the queen and co-ruler with King Asar (Osiris, Greek). Humanity's archetypal Black Madonna.
7. Two outstanding Afrikan American visionary epic poets, leaders in the 1960s Black Arts cultural era.
8. Greek for a monolithic, four sided Egyptian pillar, which tapers into a pyramid, symbolic of pharoanic authority.
9. Kemetic. The original divine bird, which served as archetype for the later Greek bird, the phoenix.
10. Divine Beings of the West Afrikan Yorubax, paralleling the Kemetic neters and the Christian/Hebrew/Muslim angels.

form a ring around your Solar Disc as
monumental love vibrations; for you are our heart, our elder sage
and parent, our cosmological thrust into parameters of Infinity,
an epiphany of Cosmic compassion
mounting summits of Divinity, an archetypal surge of Harmony
within temples of Maatic Eternity;
in Pyramids and mythic shadows, in sunbursts and meteor showers,
we wish you long life in transcendental vistas
amid pristine solos raising the Dead;
We ask that Ra, mounting
His Barque of Millions of Years, welcome His son
into infinite realms of joy, Mansions
of the Cosmic Light!

Imani[1] in Sunburst Summer: A Chant

Perhaps one morning the sky will be
turquoise speckled with gold, and I
will walk my lonely, warrior's stride
down sepia West End streets—in early
June, say. Nothing unusual in the day;
black crowds milling about in eternity,
as usual. Myriad Afrikans needing love,
joy, companionship—slowly dying inside
from lack of them, but "fronting," like
everything is "cool." Yes, a normal
Atlanta morning in our World. Maybe I'll
stop by "Life's Essentials"[2] for a quick
ginger beer, or delicious apple pie—
and you'll be there. Nothing unusual,
no blaring trumpets, or romantic mood
music, nothing except a voice speaking
with electric inflections, as I turn
to face your special magic, honey woman
of Yoruba myth: your sepia warmth,
large ashe[3] eyes, and elegant lips
of Afrikan classics claiming me, in
dreamtones supreme. And the Day becomes

1. A Swahili word meaning faith, which is often a female name.
2. A popular, Africentric health food store located in Atlanta's colorful West End 'hood.
3. A Yoruba term, meaning "let it be so," but associated with the magical aspects of making things happen; hence, ashe eyes.

special in intensity, explosive with
implications: a song somewhere burning
saxophones against the steady drums'
heartbeat; a "yes" to chants in memory's
potential, accenting sunburst gold
in your loppa[4] embracing voluptuous hips;
and the dance enjoined for myriad
lifetimes begins, as simply as my arms
wrapped around your slender waist!

4. A long, graceful wrap-around skirt worn by Afrikan women, usually of beautiful, vivid colors.

Natasha Trethewey

Natasha Trethewey was born in Gulfport, Mississippi, in 1966. A member of the Dark Room Collective, her poems have appeared in Agni, Callaloo, Gettysburg Review, The Massachusetts Review, *and* The Southern Review.

Domestic Work, 1937

All week she's cleaned
someone else's house,
stared down her own face
in the shine of copper-
bottomed pots, polished
wood, toilets she'd pull
the lid to—that look saying

Let's make a change, girl.

But Sunday mornings are hers—
church clothes starched
and hanging, a record spinning
on the console, the whole house
dancing. She raises the shades,
washes the rooms in light,
buckets of water, Octagon soap.

Cleanliness is next to godliness . . .

Windows and doors flung wide,
curtains two-stepping
forward and back, neck bones
bumping in the pot, a choir
of clothes clapping on the line.

Nearer my God to thee . . .

She beats time on the rugs,
blows dust from the broom
like dandelion spores, each one
a wish for something better.

Secular

Work-week's end and there's enough
block-ice in the box
to chill a wash tub of colas
and one large melon, dripping green.
After service, each house opens
heavy doors to street and woods—
one clear shot from front to back,
bullet, breeze, or holler.
A neighbor's *Yoo hoo* reaches her
out back, lolling, pulling in wash,
pillow slips billowing—her head
in the clouds.

Up the block, a brand new graphanola,
parlor music, blues parlando—Big Mama,
Ma Rainey, Bessie—*baby shake that thing*
like a salt shaker. Lipstick, nylons
and she's out the door, tipping past
the church house. Dixie Peach
in her hair, greased forehead shining
like gospel, like gold.

Naola Beauty Academy, New Orleans, Louisiana, 1943

Made hair? The girls here
put a press on your head
last two weeks. No naps.

They learning. See the basins?
This where we wash. Yeah,
it's hot. July jam.

Stove always on. Keep the combs
hot. Lee and Ida bumping hair
right now. Best two.

Ida got a natural touch.
Don't burn nobody.
Her own's a righteous mass.

Lee, now she used to sew.
Her fingers steady
from them tiny needles.

She can fix some bad hair.
Look how she lay them waves.
Light, slight and polite.

Not a one out of place.

Drapery Factory, Gulfport, Mississippi, 1956

She made the trip daily, though
later she would not remember
how far to tell the grandchildren—
better that way.
She could keep those miles
a secret, and her black face
and black hands, and the pink bottoms
of her black feet
a minor inconvenience.

She does remember the men
she worked for, and that often
she sat side by side
with white women, all of them
bent over, pushing into the hum
of the machines, their right calves
tensed against the pedals.

Her lips tighten speaking
of quitting time when
the colored women filed out slowly
to have their purses checked,
the insides laid open and exposed
by the boss's hand.

But then she laughs
when she recalls the soiled Kotex
she saved, stuffed into a bag

in her purse, and Adam's look
on one white man's face, his hand
deep in knowledge.

Collection Day

Saturday morning, Motown
forty-fives and thick seventy-eights
on the phonograph, window fans
turning light into our rooms,
we clean house to a spiral groove,
sorting through our dailiness—
washtubs of boiled-white linens,
lima beans soaking, green as luck,
trash heaped out back for burning—
everything we can't keep,
make new with thread or glue.

Beside the stove, a picture calendar
of the seasons, daily scripture,
compliments of the Everlast Interment
Company, one day each month marked
in red—PREMIUM DUE—collection visit
from the insurance man, his black suits
worn to a shine. In our living room
he'll pull out photos of our tiny plot,
show us the slight eastward slope,
all the flowers in bloom now, how neat
the shrubs are trimmed, *and see here,*
the trees we planted are coming up fine.

We look out for him all day, listen
for the turn-stop of wheels
and rocks crunching underfoot.
Mama leafs through the Bible
for our payment card—June 1969,
the month he'll stamp PAID
in bright green letters, putting us
one step closer to what we'll own,
something to last: patch of earth,
view of sky.

Hot Comb

Halfway through an afternoon
of coca cola bottles sweating rings
on veneered tabletops and the steel drone
of window fans above the silence
in each darkened room, I open a stiff drawer
and find the old hot combs, black
with grease, the teeth still pungent
as burning hair. One is small, fine toothed
as if for a child. Holding it,
I think of my mother's slender wrist,
the curve of her neck as she leaned over
the stove, her eyes shut as she pulled
the wooden handle and laid flat the wisps
at her temples. The heat in our kitchen
made her glow that morning I watched her
wincing, the hot comb singeing her brow,
sweat glistening above her lips,
her face made strangely beautiful
as only suffering can do.

Quincy Troupe

Quincy Troupe, born in 1943, is professor of creative writing and Ameri-
can and Caribbean literature at the University of California, San Diego.
He is the author of five books of poetry, including Avalanche and Snake-
Back Solos, for which he received an American Book Award in 1980. He
received a second American Book Award in 1990 for Miles: The Auto-
biography, which he coauthored. He is the two-time Heavyweight Cham-
pion of Poetry sponsored by the World Poetry Bout of Taos, New Mexico.

& Syllables Grow Wings There

a blackboard in my mind holds words eye dream—
& blessed are the words that fly like birds into poetry—
& syllables attach wings to breath & fly away there
through music, my language springing round from where
a bright polished sound, burnished as a new copper penny
shines in the air like the quick, jabbing glint of a trumpet
lick flicking images through voices there pulsating like strobe lights
the partying dark understands, as heartbeats pumping rhythms hip-
hopping through footsteps, tick-tocking like clocks with stopgap
measures of caesuras breaking breath, like california earth-
quakes trying to shake enjambed fault lines of minimalls
freeways & houses off their backs, rocks being pushed up there
by edges of colliding plates, rivers sliding down through yawning
cracks, pooling underneath speech, where worlds collide & sound cuts
deep fissures into language underneath the earth, the mystery of it all
seeded within the voodoo magic of that secret place, at the center
of boiling sound & is where poetry springs from now
with its heat of eruption, carrying volcanic lava flows of word
sound cadences, a sluiced-up voice flowing into the poem's
mysterious tongue, like magic, or fingers of fire dancing,
gaseous stick figures curling off the sun's back
& is where music comes up from, too, to improvise
like choirs of birds in springtime, when the wind's breath
turns warm & their voices riff off sweet songs, a cappella

One for Charlie Mingus

into space-time walks bass strings of charlie mingus
jambalaya rhythms deepening our ears, hear
voices springing from tongues of mingus riding sweet bass strings
deep stepping through sound, through light & shadows of blood
cut out into the leaping night walking music swings the wind
as tongues of evening caress the flying darkness, there
inside rhythms, tight embraces of sound-thump bass grooves
lengthening the graceful flights of cadences shading chords of voodoo
who doing who there, juicing mean watts boys sluicing, shimmy down
mean streets of the city of angels, when mingus played a strange
        disquieting
beauty, turned it on, believed in whatever he thought he was back then
played it all the way here, where eye am dreaming now, listening
within this moment of musical amazement, walking in
his voice riding in through vibrating strings thumping & humping
like naked lovers inside musky hot steaming rumpled backwater bedrooms
in the afterglow undercover of damplight, in the nighttime of their dreams
mingus skybreaking his bass through steep blue
lifetimes of urban screams, who doing what to whom
inside the city of lights, raining tears, raining blood & blue showers
electrifying nights where mingus walked music through voodoo
flying all the way home, thumping the rhythms, mingus stalks
the music tone after magical tone, walks the mysterious
music all the way home, tone after magisterial tone

Avalanche

For K. Curtis Lyle & the memory of Richard Wright

within an avalanche of glory hallelujah skybreaks
spraying syllables on the run, spreading
sheets, waving holy sounds, solos sluicing african bound
transformed here in america from voodoo into hoodoo
inside tonguing blues, snaking horns, where juju grounds down sacred
up in chords, up in the gritty foofoo
magical, where fleet rounds of cadences whirlpool
as in rivers, where memory spins down foaming into dances
like storms swallowed here in a burst of suns
up in the yeasting blue voodoo, holding
the secret clues mum, inside the mystery, unfolding
up in the caking dishrag of daybreak, miracles

shaking out earthquakes of light
like mojo hands luminous with spangling
& are the vamping blood songs of call & response
are the vamping blood songs of call & response

as in the pulpit, when a preacher becomes his words
his rhythms those of a sacred bluesman, dead outside his door
his gospel intersecting with antiphonal guitars, a congregation of amens
as in the slurred riffs blues strings run back echoing themselves
answering the call, the voice cracked open like an egg, the yolk running
    out
the lungs imitating collapsed drums & he
is the rainbowing confluence of sacred tongues, the griot
the devotion of rivers all up in his hands, all up in his fingers
his call both invocation & quaking sermon
running true & holy as drumming cadences
brewed in black church choirs, glory hallelujah vowels
spreading from their mouths like wolfman's mojo
all up in mahalia jackson's lungs
howling vowels rolled off hoodoo consonants, brewing
magic all up in the preacher's run, of muddy water
strung all up in the form drenched with coltrane
riffin' all up in miles of lightning hopkins mojo songs
blues yeasting lungs of bird
when music is raised up as prayer & lives
healing as june's sun quilted into black babies
tongues, sewn deep in their lungs as power
& blueprinted here in breath of rappers

& this is a poem in praise of continuity
is a poem about blood coursing through tongues
is a praise song for drowned voices lost in middle passage
is a praise song for the slashed drums of obatala
is a construct of orikis linking antiphonal bridges
is a praise song tonguing deep in the mojo secrets of damballah
in praise of the great god's blessings of oshun
in praise of healing songs sewn into tongues
inflating sweet lungs into a cacophony of singing
praise songs tonguing deep mojo secrets

& this poem is about music, when music is what it believes
it is, holy, when voices harmonize, somersaulting
in flight, & glory is the miracle poetry sings to in that great getting-up

morning, within the vortex of wonder, confluencing rivers, light,
glory in the rainbows arching like eyebrows across suns
glory in the moonlight staring from a one-eyed cat's head
& eye want to be glory & flow in that light
want to be coltrane's solos living in me
want to become wonder of birds in flight of my lines
want the glory of song healing in me as sunlight
want it tongued through leaves
metaphoring trees, transformed where they seed & stand up here
as people, in this soil, everything rooted here in blood of mother's flesh
& is the poetry of god in deep forest time, singing & listening
& the music there is green, as it also is purple
as it also is orange brown & mind-blowing electric banana
as it is red cinnamon & also again green
sound ground up against lavender
beneath sunsets fusing crisp blue light
& night here stitched with fireflies flicking
gold up against bold midnight & once again, yes,
green, as shimmering caribbean palm fronds
are green in the center of apocalyptic chaos

& my poem here is reaching for that greenness
is reaching for holy luminosity shimmering in gold-
flecked light, where the mojo hand is seaming through
high blue mornings, waving like a sequined glove up in the glory
of hallelujahs, calling through the innertube lips of the great god
singing, up in the blues root doctors, jacklegging sermons
up in the condolences mourning death
up in the sunburst of god's glory
& eye want this poem to kneel down itself before healing
want it to be magic there beneath the crucifixion of light
want it to be praise song, juju rooted
want it to be mojo hand raised up to powers of flight
want it to be tongue of gritty foofoo, feeding
want it to be a congregation slurring amen riffs
running back through me to you
the voice raised up here, guitar blues licks, holy
want it to be glory hallelujah, call & response, glory
want it to be yam song rooted in the bloody river, holy
want it to be ground earth of resurrection, in you, in me
the bridge tongue of healing is the drum of this song
& it is reaching out to you to cross over
to the sun, is reaching out to touch your heartbeat

there, to become one in the glory
to feel the healing touch
to become one with the glory
this poem waits for you to cross over
to cross over the heartbeat touch of your healing
hands, touching hands, touching hearts
this poem waits for you to cross over
to cross over love, this poem waits for you
to cross over, to cross over love
this poem waits for you to crossover
too crossover, too, love

Frank X. Walker

Frank X. Walker was born in Danville, Kentucky, in 1961. He is a found-
ing member of the Affrilachian Poets and the Bluegrass Arts Consortium.
He is also program coordinator of the University of Kentucky's M. L King
Jr. Cultural Center and a creative writing instructor for the Kentucky Gov-
ernor's School for the Arts. Recent publishing credits include the Appala-
chian Journal, My Brother's Keeper: An Anthology of African American
Male Poets, and Shooting Star Review.

Wishbone

often times
parents
at that fork in the road
grab on to their end
like the smallest part of the wishbone
close their eyes
and snap
and wish
nothing but pain and suffering
and revenge
on their now severed halves
the used to be
til death do us part kiss me lips
now scream
kiss my ass
and you can raise those snotty nosed kids
by yourself
iron will
and skillets
answered with such venom
that he left
believing
only a crazy man would have stayed
though he never saw
the butcher's knife
that was stopped in its path
by the back door he slammed
for the last time

he never looked back
at the puddle of woman
he had snatched
from a high school honors program
and awarded apron strings
traded her diploma for
two thousand one hundred and ninety days
in a roll of diaper duty
instead
he sprouted wings
and carried all of his paycheck
to another nest
took off his shoes
in a prettier place
with nicer things
a place un-littered with crumb snatchers
and pretended that he never
gave his name away
never said i do
never looked back

thirty years later
he stands much shorter
than his photograph
and moves without the same decisiveness
that used to carry him out
of the same stores
or into a backroom
if we were sent to visit
on his payday

granny always said
he'd come crawling back
mamma said
she couldn't wait that long
and gave her love and
four more kids
to a man
who made her feel young
again

often times
parents

mammas and pappas
at that fork in the road
grab on to their end
like the smallest part
of the wishbone
close their eyes
and snap.

Crooked Afro

daddy don't smile
when you ask 'bout
uncle jay
my favorite
drunk or sober

unk got bookoo years
fo' shootin'
a man
inna club

some say
he didn't do it
that he took the rap
for his brotha
my father
who had three of us
in diapers

this man's man
had already done time
in 'nam
wasn't back but a minute
when this other
tour of duty
called

a stretch in eddiville
would be nuthin'
but a slow dance
he said

but when he tripped home
one easter
to his father's funeral
and stood at the coffin in cuffs
the music stopped

when we welcomed him back
he came to the party
without his dancing shoes
his record skipping
singing a song
that old lovers
and ex teammates
had already put in the attic

now half of him
and a crooked afro
roam the streets
and alleys
borrowing just enough
for another bottle
to make love to

hoping to find somebody
who still listens
to isaac hayes or
little stevie wonder
on eight tracks
and remembers when
he could just take over a game
if the bate bulldogs
were behind
and the cheerleaders
called his name

daddy don't smile
when you ask 'bout uncle jay
and some of us
still cry
when he tries to dance.

Sweet Bread

singing his name
in a tongue he didn't understand
wishing him husband
she knew she'd never have
she found him
in the darkness
every night
rubbed his anger
to sleep
gifted him
with bread crumbs
and dried fruit
liberated from above

aboard his manhood
cursing the chains
that prevented him from holding her
she rode
and cried
rode
and laughed
rode
and made a home for his seed
every night
mocking the death
that rode with them
mocking the strange pale ones
with stone eyes and hands
that rode her and passed her
and filled her mouth
with manskin
at knifepoint

she knelt and swallowed
stuffing her pockets with table scraps
rubbing honey
on her breast
honey
hardened by ocean sun
that when set
would mix

with salt water
tears
and become
sweetbread
for a lover
she could smell
a deck away.

Jackie Warren-Moore

Jackie Warren-Moore, born in 1950, is a poet, playwright, and news columnist. Based in Syracuse, she is on the staff of the Community Writers' Project. Her work appears in Sisterfire: Black Womanist Fiction and Poetry.

For Paula Cooper
(The 18 year old who waits on death row)

Paula of the trembling brown cheeks and silent tears
I see you struggling and stumbling
day leaning into day.
Seasons and years measured by the shadows on the walls and the
metal clang of lockup,
Death and fifteen years of abuse bearing down on you.
Hungry and wanting you plunged the knife.
Like a sacrificial lamb, did you think her blood would wash clean
the misery of your life?
33 times you twisted and plunged into another's life.
Still the freedom did not come. The pain did not end.
Only the time of waiting continues.
Waiting for a kind word. Waiting for the abuse to end. Waiting to
be wanted. Waiting to be loved. Waiting for a time there will be
no waiting. Waiting to die convulsing in the electric chair.
Paula of the soft brown cheeks and silent tears,
Wishing you laughter and 18 year old joy.
Wishing you a decision no harder than what dress to wear to the Prom.
Hungry and wanting.
I see you on streetcorners throughout the country. The same soft
brown cheeks and silent tears.
I see you in the faces of a generation left waiting.
Like a sacrificial lamb, I see you
Silent silver streaks flowing down baby brown cheeks.
Waiting.

For Etheridge Knight

I learned of your death over spiced tea
with my breath blowing against

the thin membrane of the academic circle,
the one constantly turning in on itself.

I sat through polite and grammatically correct conversations
a full rundown of all your sins.
Which actually killed you?
heroin or cocaine?
Pussy or lack thereof.

Was it your last love or the old love
newly found
that sheltered you
in the last shuddering moments.

Heard them speak about the tsk tsk trauma and
tragedy of a miserable life.
Not one motherfucking mumbling word about the passion,
about the lust for life that led
you crashing over the cliff
like the soft brown baby boy you were.
Not one note of the Coltrane riff that rode you
through the long prison nights.
Not one word of the copper thighs that wrapped
safe
from a world gone stir-crazy
Not one stanza of the academic prosody that sought to make
you abandon
the Mothertongue
Not one Motherfucking word about the bars etched indelibly
in your mind and mine.

I suck your words,
roll them bitter
across my tongue
and mourn my loss.

Dannemora Contraband

Stony lonesome reached out and grabbed me.
Surrounded me with gray walls
gun towers and fear.

Dannemora blues. Made the clouds weep buckets
on our heads.

Inside, on the count, where the young bloods walk
with a warrior's bounce,
the proud, gray haired man
speaks of the Ancestors and half
a century of long, lonely nights inside.
Inside Dannemora,
Inside himself.

Smiles weigh more in Dannemora.

Inside, a smile can soothe like mother's lullaby,
satisfy like a lover's caress,
it can bandage a wound deep and festering,
touch the primal Ancestor in us all.
Inside, a smile can share what might be missed by the faceless
passerby.
To those men surrounded by gray walls, gun towers and fear.

When the clouds open and pour buckets,
when the night wraps itself long and lonely around you.

Listen carefully to the sound behind the raindrops.
It is only me on the other side,
tossing smiles over the wall.

The All-Night Issue

An issue, with cold feet, jumped in bed with us.
Slid between us and pushed against our backs.
Warmed itself in the heat of us and chilled to the bone.
A thin, unimportant issue that spread and sprawled out,
nudged us to the opposite edges of the bed.
An issue that threw its arms around our necks,
choked and humped us into exhaustion,
dug its dry heels into all the exposed parts.
Wound itself in all the available covering while we lay apart,
exposed,
shivering,

sleepless,
speechless in silence.

Pink Poem

This is a big girl's pink poem,
a poem about pinkness.
Deep dark shadowy rose I explore at the back of your mouth.
This is not a hot pink pinafore, lacy poem.
This is a poem about the long lean pinkness of your tongue
as it greets my lips.
This is about the sweet wet melt in my mouth motion of you.
This is not about the sashay,
turn around
curtsy pink cuteness.
This is about opening up and being gloriously pink.
This is a big girl's pink poem.

Michael S. Weaver

Michael S. Weaver, born in 1952, is a native of Baltimore, Maryland. His poems have appeared in numerous journals and anthologies, and his volumes include Water Song, My Father's Geography, Stations in a Dream, *and* Timber and Prayer: The Indian Pond Poems. *He lives in Philadelphia and is on the faculty of Rutgers University, Camden.*

Sub Shop Girl

For James "Eddie" Mann

She is lovely. Her eyes are big almonds
floating over the electronic cash register.
She puts magic dust in my mayonnaise,
hoochie-koochie notes in my fries.
There is no other reason to order
tomatoes, lettuce, hot peppers, onions,
and french fries in a suit and tie.
I come nearer the shop tiptoeing in Florsheims.
With a quarter I set the mood on the jukebox.
"What do you want today?" she asks, "What is it, Baby?"
I am probably the only man who puts strategy
in a Saturday night foray to the sub shop.
I line my cologne up carefully on the dresser,
the Parisian designer bottle for cheese steak,
for pizza the cheaper, less subtle aromas,
laying my clothes out to match each meal.
She puts the change in my palm a coin at a time,
measuring the contours of the lines in my hands.
I think I lost my sanity a long time ago
on the way to buy a foot-long and fries.
The essence of Shango fires my red urge
longing to meld with the small greasy apron
that throws frozen steak portions with expertise.
How could the heavens have wasted such youth
on me and this corner sub shop and vagrants
and the empty neon in after-hours streets,
and the music from old Smokey Robinson 45's
I play on my boom box the nights I want to serenade?
Have you ever listed the extras on a cold cut with
"Tracks of My Tears" or "Second That Emotion"?

When the shop is closed some Sundays I melt
in the afternoon apparitions in the empty windows,
the deserted counters, the cold ovens, the silence.
There are blessings for noble spirits confined
to ordinary lives, the dribble of an oba like me
and a great spirit like my sub shop Oshun slicing pickles.
There are blessings as we dazzle the ordinary universe,
pervert the threadbare perceptions of doldrums
with our elegant affair at night, our perfect love,
me in an all-leather racing jacket and Gucci loafers.

One night after work I'll coax her and we'll pretend
to be Marvin Gaye and Tammi Terrell on the parking lot.
I'll caress her around the waist and spin her softly.
A dark night sky laden with stars will crack,
the moon will pour love's essence on the earth,
truth will overcome us on the voices of the orishas—
"Ain't Nothin Like the Real Thing Baby," or maybe
"You're All I Need to Get By," but most of all the song
the world needs to hear—"You Ain't Livin Till You're Lovin."
I am probably the only man who sees the answer
in a cheese-steak hoagie with all the fixins and fries,
music from my boom box or the jukebox nearby,
two almond eyes as deep as canyons over the counter,
and my Gucci and Florsheim shoes doing a soft tap,
the mania and danger of an insecure world hanging out
like a florid design in the curtain of the night.

Providence Journal V:
Israel of Puerto Rico

In the clutter and clatter of the Bronx,
your uncle's Chihuahuas tipped
over the tile floors with a song that ticked
with a rhythm like the swirl of the calabash.
You counted the day's wages from the track,
bounced your head like hands above congas.
You popped a rhythm into the living room
where the dominant music was the World Series
on the television where your uncle cheered.

At home in Humacao, your mother gave her sermon
on the dangers of Manhattan, the other island.
There women can turn a good boy like you
into the aching salsa of empty pockets,
hearts chopped down to lifeless fibers.
You nodded your head and promised to obey—
yes to your mother's wisdom, yes to her fear.
In New York your eyes turned at once
to a dance no one can see, the dance of hedonism
wrapped in care, wrapped in a mother's eye
as miraculous and far-ranging as the sun itself.

On Sunday nights we rode back to Providence.
You patted the dashboard and cried out to me,
cried out to the night that snickered outside,
"New York is sweet irony. New York is my poem."

Brooklyn
For Mizan Kirby Nunes

Over Manhattan Bridge,
I land in the breast of Brooklyn,
in the thoroughfares that slap
the earth like fresh switches
in the playful hands of children.
Once in Brooklyn I walked
with Charles, my gossip partner,
through the West Indian festival,
commenting on the floats,
watching Spike Lee sign autographs.
We saw Brooklyn raw,
stepping out of its clothes,
walking toward some conjugal laughter,
its various parts rolling, shaking
in this marvelous vanity parading.

And for my thirty-ninth birthday,
I saw a South African musical
at the Brooklyn Academy of Music,
whose acronym knocks you out.
The colors were sensational.
My wife laughed, Robert napped,

my musical gift beat itself
into the frenzy of townships
and laws that make cities
the shy strangers to their own history,
make them unsure of themselves
with identity crises that set generations
into the bumbling unraveling
of substantiating a culture's place
in the wavering world,
on the moody map.

In my father's sister's home
on the other side of Prospect Park,
I listened to tongues that flow
like bourbon, tongues that
were born in the flat perspective
of Virginia. There the trees rise
like those in a child's drawing,
the scrawling crayon signifying
the need to move up North,
to migrate, to go until something inward
sets your heart to ringing out
a shout. In my aunt's home
on Maple Street, I heard the sputter
of black souls that found Brooklyn
when the Tenderloin fell
into the conquering coffers
of greed. In Brooklyn I saw bare feet circling
in the sand and heard voices singing *home.*

Easy Living
For Dorothy West

From the shiny iron stove,
where your mother cooked,
you move to your small writing table
past the foot-high, yellow dictionary.
You remember the days your mother
took you and your rainbow cousins
out to shock the white folks.
Your mother had a cream color,

her pink cheeks against your gingersnap
brown you call an apolitical colored.

Your mother forbade you to ever
set foot in the South. She told you
about her mother, who was a slave.
This slave grandmother of yours
had eleven children by her master.
One day, a little girl who was your aunt
stepped on the tail of her white father's dog.
Your grandfather went into a rage
and he killed your grandmother's daughter.
The South still frightens you.

Your Oak Bluffs cottage sits
like a dollhouse on Myrtle Avenue.
You see an image arise.
It is your father as he sells
the restaurant in Richmond
that he opened with his mother.
He moved north to Springfield, Massachusetts,
to the produce stand that made him
Boston's black banana king and
allowed him to buy a brick house
on Brookline Avenue and the summer home
on Martha's Vineyard. He ached
to leave you more when he died,
more than the memory of his blue eyes.

Sometimes black but certainly colored,
you reminisce about your news column,
"The Cottager's Corner," where you chronicled
the island's famous colored, like
the first black college president.
Then Wallace Thurman comes to mind,
and you remember with a smile
Langston Hughes, whom you asked in a letter
to marry you—and have children with you.
You think of how he declined the offer,
and you look out the window and chuckle.
On the island there is no time for regrets.
You serve your tenure gracefully,

evidence of a world with wonders
like your small hand in Langston's
in the cold Atlantic, churning to a Russian film,
to the eye that makes the memory.

Mary Weems

Mary Weems, *born in 1954, earned her M.A. in creative writing from Cleveland State University. She was winner of the 1995 "Ohio Writer" poetry contest. She has published a chapbook entitled* Blackeyed *and was the Artistic Director for the book and video project* Off the Page.

B.B. Blues

"And if it's not askin' too much, pleeease
send me someone to love."

B.B.'s on every station
cradling Lucille in his arms
like Cupid's cold-cocked arrow. I am
Lucille, my strings pluck, breaking
across the face of the room—kitchen
table place setting gathering dust,
blood on the soup spoon. Invisible
work boots wrap me in a tight kiss.
The floor is blue, old love-talk crawls
around on blue legs. I beg it to be quiet,
silence sits in my ear.

"To know you is to love you, but
to know me is not that way it seems,"

B.B. shifts gears, my ears stick.
B.B. Blues, a foot patting croon,
made for blackeyed peas and corn bread
parties, moonshine nights, days sleeping
carefully on one-side of a one-side bed,
body tremble at 3 o'clock in the mornin'
lifting the toilet seat as a reminder,
the smell of magic shave missing the magic.

B.B. comes in blue when I want him to,
lets me run my fingers through Lucille's
hair, sit on his knee
eating and drinking blues
never full.

Yesterday

Black Mary Janes, white-ruffled sox,
hopscotch, cartoons, hide 'n seek,
were all that mattered.

Mama didn't lock our doors at night
and nobody broke in.

My yard was bigger than the whole world.

The only white person in our neighborhood
was the 25-cent-a-week insurance man.

Baseball was a flat board
and a rock.

Everybody had roaches.

40 was old as white thread.

Summer, lightnin' bugs, white butterflies,
Mr. Toe Jam, the ice cream truck man.

Time moved like clouds.

Dime after Dime

My daughter
tosses a dime in lake Erie
wishing for her father.

At eleven-years old
she carries around
a brown mailman teddy bear
because at 5,
that was the last thing
he gave her.

Holding onto secondhand
tears, I flash
to my own wash

without a teddy to cling to
only eyes like hers
and a mama who lied
about my daddy's love.

A sudden hug
catches my arms
twisting to turn
to my daughter
making a wish of my own

tossing an invisible dime.

Funk

For: T. M.

I cling to the funk
want to keep the kitchen in my hair,
suck neckbones 'til they pop,
talk shit with my girlfriends,
eat Alaga syrup and granny's biscuits
with my fingers, smell press 'n curl
hair in a beauty shop on Saturday afternoon,
stand around in my yard sayin' mothafucka this
and mothafucka that laughin' at shit that's funny
just because you jivin', dip in somebody's business
and play the dozens for about a hour,
find somebody who remembers "the signifyin' monkey,"
go dancin', shakin' my booty and sweatin' until my feet hurt,
and I smell like cheap wine, listen to
B.B. King, Miles, the Funkadelic, and the Temptin'
Temptations, singin' all the words off-key, forget
about everything else 'cept how good it is to be
black.

Return to Temptation

After hearing about the death of Melvin
Franklin, of the Temptations.

Melvin's dead,
a cloud-nine moves

a 4-step sway to the left
in 5-part harmony,
the sun shines at half-mast,
silent nights have a fit.

Melvin's dead.
I am 13 again
sitting in new beginner
bra, first stockings
and heels, facing
the stage at Leo's Casino
holding my breath.
The space darkens and David,
doo glistening like black
magic, sequined lapel flashing
moonlight, steps up letting a smooth
note float from a mouth
made for singing.
"Sonny," and Temptation
fills the room
like new money.
I watch, throat dry
as fall leaves, as Eddie,
Melvin, Otis, and Paul
fall into steps so together
they are one movement.

Melvin's dead.
The psychedelic shack opens,
filled with spirits
chanting
"psychedelic shack that's where it's at
psychedelic shack that's where it's at"
champagne popping corks
like banana-brown fingers,
punch spiked
with shaking boodies
and doo-wops bubbling.

Melvin's dead.
I want to ride
on Ol' Man River
carve out a canoe

bare fingers bleeding
yesterday.
Paddle into his heart
pump it up
pump it up
pump it up
so full of love
it rises.
Grab one of them 9 lives
God gives cats
on a regular basis
so Melvin can get
back in line
back in step
let out a single
note—
return to
Temptation.

Karen Williams

Karen Williams was born in 1962. A staff member at a Metro Detroit health department, she has been published in Inner Visions, *an anthology released by the Detroit Black Writers Guild, and in such publications as* Iconoclast, Sophomore Jinx, *and* Negative Capability Journal.

Little Black Girls, The Original Eve
(Spreadin' More Beautiful Brown Around)

A
Bodacious
 Black
  Bad
   Beautiful
    Beguiling celebration
of verve, curves
raw naked nerve
spreads her
     beautiful
      black
       strong
on the cutting edge legs
and breathes, heaves
clutches the heavens
and gives birth to
     beautiful
      brown seeds
of ingenuity
each time
she gives birth to
  Black
   Beautiful
    Female
     Me

    The Original Eve

destined to spring
from her
  Beautiful

Black
loins
to incubate
give birth
to more of her
Beautiful
Black
seed

Little Black girls
One of the true joys of motherhood

There's History in My Hair

I once read a poem
about the politics of hair
then afterwards looked in the mirror
and wondered when I was little
in my coal colored halo of kink and frizzle
did a prevailing stick straight world
see a nappy, ugly me

I mean could they see all the way to Africa in my eyes
my nakedness, my culture exposed enough for them
to wish they had a missionary at hand
to civilize, sanctify me
a little girl who proudly wielded a pink ace comb
and volunteered at school
to comb their naturally silky hair

I was young
called it playing beauty shop
only realizing years later
even then, how beautiful I was
with my tawny skin unlike crushed pearls
my mahogany eyes more deep, sparkling
than those blue as cerulean skies
where across flew the bird of privilege, paradise

I was young, then
a fledgling phoenix still waiting to be born
and to think all this came

from reading a poem
from examining the politics
of my skin and hair
and realizing
even as a happy, nappy little girl
how phenomenal
   how compelling
      how infinite
         my beauty was

and still is

In My Grandmother's Living Room

With you I learned my part in nature
beamed like B.B.'s blues into your pristine living room
during immeasurable nights of Mutual of Omaha's Wild Kingdom,
the deep sea dives of Jacques Cousteau,
the oddly familiar clamor of African tongues on PBS
sunny days of Big Bird on Sesame Street.

Remember how we bristled at a gravelly globe-trotting George Perot?
Few remember him now,
his contemplation of reaching your dreams
then seemingly boarding a plane with open one-way ticket,
always to find them.
You taught me in our tiny town
filled with whites, blacks, indiscriminate blues
like George and Bald Eagles I could fly
without leaving the breadbox warmth of your house
surrounded by blooms of swiss chard and collards
I'd tend with you each summer.

And remember how we scraped those stubborn scales from
grandfather's sea-sweet fish?
I'd pinch my nose and look at you in awe.
You knew what you were doing, were never afraid,
just grabbed him by the tail and scraped away with gusto.
His firm white flesh would tease the palate,
serve you and our family well.
Only you could teach me that,
that over, underneath and surrounding our brownness

the most simple things, simple forms, and simple people
are uncharted discoveries, unique jewels,
bold new perspectives, worlds like sweet fruit to be found.

You also taught me God's glory wasn't limited to Whites.
Wasn't limited at all to those whose houses you cleaned.
I could find it, you said, in your strong and gentle arms,
beyond mountains of chicken waiting to be plucked and fried,
and forever beyond the panes of your always open door.

Ntarama (Rwanda) Chronicles

Part I

In sandblows once green,
amid dust, flies, cholera's cornet,
sweet children play, unknowing creatures born, nursed,
nurtured by a The Omniscient as Hutu machete's slice
beseeching hands seeking instruction, solace in His house.
"Hail Mary's" defer to bleeding pews and decades,
barrens growing lush with a child's blushing thoughts
of Mother's morning kiss, her lifeblood entering
souls of Her children later to seek secret saviours,
secret places to mourn.

Part II

Skulls stacked neatly as stones
at the foot of cool brick, bleached
from non-absolving heat as "Amazing Grace"
blooms in Rwadian tongues among crabgrass,
prostrate kin to craniums crushed,
the tissue, blood, hopes of the dead,
rust colored stains on clothing-wound pews
where ought to sit Hutu sinners, their
sabers of self-hatred eternally fixed in
Excalibur's stone.

For Backwards Buppies

We are bemoaned, befuddled, bespectacled
balls of confusion

driving our beamers
trying to buy, appreciate bows
tying our psyches into subconscious knots,
relaxed kinks, moats, sink holes
heaps of convention, collective ignorance

Avowed intellectuals
we fail to know ourselves
hold titles, propers, degrees
but still don't know shit
the meaning behind diaries and letters because our vocabularies
are so big, so booming, so becoming
we look just like fools trapped spouting words
ranting schemas, dogmas, philosophies, isms
we can't diffuse, define or understand

We are balls of confusion
hold no bombs or real surprises
are the flotsam, the jetsam of the turbulent 60's
the flower-filled, funky, free your mind and ass 70's
we aren't down for any cause
are too young or stupid to know about 'Nam
say loudly I'm Black and I'm proud
but secretly covet the boss or his daughter
we embrace Walter Williams destinies
dream of Telluride, diamonds and furs
get a rush out of fools named Limbaugh
think of humping, bumping, more money
are small fish lost in a big pond
never heard of Saint Louis, Saint James or Goree
are too busy to trip and soar on the Continent
and find our natural selves

We are balls of confusion
have forgotten who we are
haven't a clue where we're going
really don't want to belong
we define ourselves in degrees,
by length and texture of our weaves
or the zeros in front of our decimals
as we trip over our ferragamoed feet
sink in sandy Cancun soil
have kissed off the work of Alex

toss our roots into rising piles we expel
from our mouths, our postures, our behinds

We are balls of confusion
are to dumb to value the rich compost of our debris
where we'll find our warp and weave
amongst hot sauce bottles, grandmother's wisdom
and as Maya says in the dreams and hopes of slaves.

JAZZ (a new interpretation)

Slick
silky
soul
with a
little bit of scat
thrill
trills
rolls
dips
and talkin shit

Shoo be do be do wop she bop
                she bop
                        she bop

YEAH

That's jazz
Euphony as brilliant as pomade on Nat Kings hair
It's a hip symphony
a quartet
a sextet
a solo of velvet smooth
it always sings
It always swings high
                swings low

Coming for to carry me
somewhere dark and always funky

Niama Leslie JoAnn Williams

Niama Leslie JoAnn Williams was born in 1962 and raised in Los Angeles, California. She is a Ph.D. student in the African American Studies Department of Temple University. Her poetry and prose has appeared in Afro-American Poetry '93, *and* River Crossings, *among other publications.*

Merging

i long for purple kisses
kisses i don't have to wet my lips for
kisses that come after a sweaty night of lovemaking
kisses that make my tongue tired
and my nipples rise.

i want to dance with you
and feel your stomach on mine
lie with you and feel the musk rise from your skin
lie with you at my back, our knees touching.

i want to taste your chest
swallow your insides as i lick the sweat from your skin
i want to bite off little pieces of you
and hide them for safekeeping.
i want to hear your voice over the phone and moan in agreement to all of
        your
questions
i want the dog not to be able to tell our scents apart.
i want to mingle our blood in an ancient rite of passage
then tend your wounds with my tongue.
i want to drink the sight of you in long, small sips
then wiggle you against my teeth.

i want your heart to share my ribcage
and your stomach to digest my food
i want to wake up tasting what you ate for dinner
i want to wake up and not tell my sweat from yours

i want an eternity together, love.

Afrocentricity

For molefi

the birth of an idea is violent

as eddie b. and sara sweated beneath the hanging tree
it formed
as douglass dreamed of freedom
it planned
as Dubois wrote of our souls
it wept
and then took aim and shot
on richard wright's page

shooting still it lingers
the wounded watch the X caps proliferate
and tell the lawyer kente is forbidden in court.
the wounded, falling, see the blackening of the college campus, the
        boardroom, the
playing field
and help our athletes graduate with no degree

shooting itself in the foot
it watches its children bicker
sees itself written about, fearfully, by its own

it has gotten bigger than itself
but comes down to this:
it puts braids on straightened hair
puts joromis on brown bodies
puts dreadlocks in boardrooms
and allows teachers to wear t-shirts that say:
"I have a right to be hostile
My people are being persecuted!"

i write this in a book of african textiles
in a room of diasporan african books.
i have read a ninety-two page paper
that cited only african scholars.
my magazines are essence and emerge
i read black and like it.

the idea swims in a very white sea
is stepped upon

stamped out
but does not die.
it saves lives with every piece of kente
with every lock blowing in the wind

many have died to allow this idea its fruition
many sacrifice souls, wisdom, courage
but it feeds on knowledge
on bright young faces
bright young brown faces
it relies not on double-consciousness,
which is deceit,
but on african consciousness
which is self-love

we turn to kemet for our origins because we too wish to be educated
like the ancient greeks
and as more of us go to home there
its strength grows.

we keep a fire banked for the idea here at temple
we warm ourselves by this fire as we stoke it
feed it our negativity, our self-hatred, our deceit
and laugh as they go up in flames.
the idea sharpens our weapons
brightens our minds
eases our weary spirits.

do not mistake us:
we are soldiers.
this is war.
we fight to clear our heads
sharpen our purpose
nurture our young
and carry the idea home
to those who wear the kente cloth
in ignorance.

For the Dancer
(kariamu keeps coming . . .)

the hand waves gracefully
silently

and all gather
as the sun delays its setting
to hear the tales of a diasporan woman
come home.

shy, she does not speak—
she moves.
movement is her voice.
she has watched her audience approach
settle themselves
and thus knows them intimately
movement is her language.

her silent screams are offstage
not for public consumption
but they are there in the grace of her dance
her fluid fight for control against the drum
the submission of her cupped hands as she thanks the drummer
who toys with her when she tries to be serious
other than the dancer that she is.

her lectures fall short
of the warm sweat on her neck
after a dance
her tongue cannot compete
with the way she cups her hips
tucks her stomach under
in a movement the villagers understand.
that single movement
and the particular warmth of her sweat
tell the villagers she is home.

on the far continent
a young woman watches her with love
it will be her duty to kiss that sweaty neck
and welcome it, and the dancer
to her new cocoon

to tell her—also with movement—
it is alright to feel more at home with the drum
than the lectern.

but the author of this poem
a diasporan woman too

for whom movement is difficult, ungainly
begs permission to fly with words the dancer has laid on the page
the aesthetic—
the polyconscious—
this poet wishes to fly
with concepts that bring the village across the seas
unbound
and wishes to witness the next time that hand halts the sun
and the cupped hips remind a villager
a lost daughter has returned.

The Meaning of the Smell of Sweat

it has been so long oshun
depression silenced your voice
walled me in
i took refuge under the covers.

now it is as though the world has started anew
i have energy again
faith again
poems bloom at 4am again
i accept that i am a night person
long for residence in a quiet town
with a theatre
where gunshots do not populate the night.

waking from depression is not a process
one morning or evening you just realize the bad days are over
suddenly you want to get out of bed
your chosen career is no longer a mistake
under the covers is no longer the safest place.

waking from depression is a gift
the doctor reduces your medication
you find you are closer to the goal line than you thought
getting a phd seems viable

you pull your head from beneath the covers and smell flowers
instead of your own sweat.

Demetrice A. Worley

Demetrice A. Worley was born in 1960 and grew up in Chicago. She received a Doctor of Arts degree from Illinois State University and has coedited an anthology, African American Literature. *She is director of Teaching Excellence Programs and teaches African American literature, creative writing, and technical writing at Bradley University.*

Tongues in My Mouth

Tired of waiting for me,
my ancestors' spirits are lifting
my heavy tongue, forming
words in my mouth.

Sa koon ain je gun,[1] my maternal
great-great grandmother's Blackfeet voice,
the light of her soul, locates my words.

*Tuwa wasteicillia maka kin lecela
tehan yunkelo,*[2] my paternal
great-great grandmother's Sioux voice,
guides me beyond concern for self.

*Asiyefunzwa na mamye hufunzwa
na ulimwengu,*[3] my foremothers'
Swahili voices, tell me listen,
hear the wisdom.

My ancestors are making me
practice my languages,
forcing me to make foreign sounds,
to turn new words over,
until the tongues in my mouth
speak in a single voice,
until the tongues in my mouth,
speak the truth that no one wants to hear.

1. Bright-white-flamed-instrument.
2. Whoever considers themselves beautiful, on earth, only endures.
3. The child who is not taught by her mother, will be taught by the world.

Dancing in the Dark

At an English conference presentation,
77 people and I breathe molecules

from Julius Caesar's last dying breath.
This is the only connection between us.

I am in a herringbone tweed suit.
Gray and black cross-hatch pattern confines

my hips, chest, back. Hair twisted,
tight coil, no loose ends escaping.

Small pearl earrings, one in each ear,
match the thin strand around my neck.

I present papers in white academia,
matching their foreign movements.

My jerky fox trot is invisible to them.
They see a waltz of standard diction:

"She speaks so well for a black woman."
One or two others like me,

dancing to a rhythm they can't hear,
smile, nod, exchange partners.

I return home, shed herringbone layer,
run hands over warm caramel skin,

wide hips, small breasts, ashy knees.
Put my hair in thick braids.

Muddy Waters on the box.
Soul slow dances back into my body.

Las Flores para una Niña Negra

I.
They make love in his first language;

he teaches only in his second language.
What else is a puertorriqueño to do?

As he sings Colombian jazz songs, he beats
a rhythm on her buttocks, her back, her belly.
She catches words—papeles, amor, revolución.

She asks for her story, "Las Flores para
una Niña Negra." In español and ingles
he whispers the story in her ear.

Una niña negra is hungry. It has
swallowed her until only her eyes,
limpid brown, exist in her face.

Her mamá tells her to sleep. In her dreams
her mamá will bring tortillas, hot and crisp.
Plump grains of rice, red beans in a spicy sauce.

Una niña negra closes her eyes, sleeps.
When she awakes, her mamá gives
her las flores, flores muy bonitas,

brilliant yellow and red flowers
from her garden. They finish.
He kisses the swell of her earlobe.

II.
Between scenes he quotes lines
from movies, *B* movies she has never seen.
He laughs because she believes his words.

He considers her admissions of naïveté
a challenge. He smiles before working
her up politically: can't she tell

the difference between Reagan and Marx?
She knows only *Masterplots.* He sighs.
He can no longer watch the movies.

The images are all translucent, and no amount
of complaining to theater owners seems to change
them. The other images he knows are real:

With care, a twelve-year-old boy balances
a small white box on his head,
as younger brothers and sisters,

the survivors, skip through the thin dust,
moving in single file towards the cemetery.
No adults accompany them.

Too many have been lost to hunger
and disease for this one to earn
an hour off from the sugar cane plantation.

Children bury children too small to labor
in the fields. In time they will learn
to grieve quickly, get on with living.

Her lover says he will be a Marxist
until oppressed people no longer exist.
He kisses her full on the mouth.

Sandra

crack has overtaken your immune defenses,
entered your endocrine system,
broken down cellular walls,

crystallized in cerebral fluid.
In your life my voice does not register.
You answer my questions with nods,

tell me, "Girl, I always wanted
to be like you." Pat my hand.
Dimpled fingers surround ragged edges

of chewed nails. Your life burns
like the fuel driven mitochondrion
in your cells, consuming energy to survive

Jesus' monthly demands for your check.
Your life governed by the Department
for Dependent Children. One last warning.

thirty more days locked in St. Luke,
as if those future days even exist,
as if you functioned on a calendar.

Your life operates like a twisted
DNA molecular strand, spinning
toward infinity, fate laid out

on a thin line—an order
scientists are beginning to understand.
Does it matter? In your life

you've let go, of yourself,
of your children—Rachel, sixteen
with a woman's hips, desires;

Maria, ten, sucking her thumb;
Paul, four, roly-poly, he laughs
only at the sound of your voice.

Al Young

Al Young, born in 1939, is based in the San Francisco Bay area. His volumes of poetry include Dancing, The Song Turning Back into Itself, Geography of the Near Past, *and* Straight No Chaser. *He performs worldwide, both solo and to jazz.*

Blue Monday

The blues blow in their purity
more than minds; blues blow
through every sky and haunted heart
afloat. They say: I miss you, baby,
so I really went out and got drunk.

Blues say: Fool that I am, I jam
you in my toaster burning-brown
like bread on fire, blackening
in the Afro-red Cadillac flame of love.

Blues say: Baby, you supposed to *be.*
Blues say: You supposed to be so big,
so bad, so slick. Quick! Tell me,
what is the distance from your heart
      to your dick?

Ravel: Bolero

Unraveling Ravel is no longer a secret;
it's all how you plop yourself
in the Spanishness of all this French
kissing in public

Dance!
That's what they say—the flute,
the muter of emotions older than time,
can dance itself.
Clarinet me that one,
Mister Tromborrorooney.

297

Ay, the clean, brown plains and slopes
of Spain forever Spain forever gallant
forever picaresque.

Saxophone says: I got your pictures;
I got my angles on all of this
and you're all full of steam—

Love is neither now nor
has it ever been tender;
it's castanets; it's the gypsy
of forever who takes you for a ride,
        my friend,
and hits you up for keeps.

Written in Bracing, Gray
L.A. Rainlight

It seems to be the time of bad gigs,
low pay, no-pay and no-shows.
Even the weary palms that line thin air-
port arcades aren't buying this light.
Busted, sleepy, hungry and blank,
the I who was, am ready for take-off.

Heaven after all is right next door;
its chilling warmth alive in time
to the swish and meter of longed-for rain
in our fourth long year of drought.
True, everybody talking about heaven
ain't going there. But if I ever
get my hands on good money again,
the price of light is going to rise
and shine. And, hear me, I ain't paying.

Fifty-Fifty
For Donald S. Ellis

By fifty, you know who you are and, more,
you almost know what you don't know. Perhaps.
You know your body-house—its roof, its floor;

know what it lacks, its leaks, its loose backsteps.
And sometimes, up alone, safe in the dark;
a Friday dinner savored, jazz, some beers—
the livingroom your camp, sweet home your park—
you drowse and dream. Remembering the dares
the younger you fulfilled without a flinch,
you picture where your children will grow old.
On 21st Century turf, each one will inch
by inch construct some crazy, brave household.
You wonder what they'll have or know of you,
who took six decades learning what to do.

The One Snapshot I Couldn't Take in France

Shot through with silver gray light,
waylaid by big-bellied bridges,
this France is not for sale. Not this
Paris, where they serve nothing but French
classics at the Polidor in Rue Monsieur
Le Prince, Richard Wright's favorite.
Hell, he lived right up the street.
We talking about the Paris where you get on
the bus and the draft you feel ain't coming
from no open windows. And while you sit,
soaking up aisle light and the street-lit faces
of passengers, you know you're neither welcome
nor wanted. Excusez-moi! Oui, you're the waif.
Your heart is busy feeling up the back pages
of places faraway, your mental roadblocks;
atlases Ayn Rand could've never shrugged off.

Kevin Young

Kevin Young, born in 1970, received the Academy of American Poets Prize
while a student at Harvard University. His work has appeared in Kenyon
Review, Ploughshares, and Poetry, as well as in other journals and an-
thologies. His first book, Most Way Home, was published by William
Morrow as part of the National Poetry series.

Reward

RUN AWAY from this sub-
scriber for the second time
are TWO NEGROES, viz. SMART,
an outlandish dark fellow

with his country marks
on his temples and bearing
the remarkable brand of my
name on his left breast, last

seen wearing an old ragged
negro cloth shirt and breeches
made of fearnought; also DIDO,
a likely young wench of a yellow

cast, born in cherrytime in this
parish, wearing a mixed coloured
coat with a bundle of clothes,
mostly blue, under her one good

arm. Both speak tolerable plain
English and may insist on being
called Cuffee and Khasa respect-
ively. Whoever shall deliver

the said goods to the gaoler
in Baton Rouge, or to the Sugar
House in the parish, shall receive
all reasonable charges plus

a genteel reward besides what
the law allows. In the mean
time all persons are strictly
forbid harbouring them, on pain

of being prosecuted to the utmost
rigour of the law. Ten guineas
will be paid to any one who can
give intelligence of their being

harboured, employed, or enter-
tained by a white person upon
his sentence; five on conviction
of a black. All Masters of vessels

are warned against carrying them
out of state, as they may claim
to be free. If any of the above
Negroes return of their own

accord, they may still be for-
given by

ELIZABETH YOUNG.

Southern University, 1962

For my father

Let's see   first afros I saw   were on these girls from
               SNCC   they had dark
berets with FREEDOM NOW on them   that barely
               covered their helmets
of hair   they sang of the struggle   of the non violent
               demonstration   in town
that weekend   By Saturday it was raining like hell   me
               and Greene
we were home boys   from Opelousas High   we were
               trying to pour in
the last of the blue and white buses this black man in
               town   had let SNCC use

I had my arm in the door   trying to get on out of the
                rain   and so split my
fiveninetyfive raincoat   right down the side   I tossed it
                on the ground
and me and Greene got on just before the bus pulled
                away   When we got
outside campus   ten big beefy white guys   with red
                faces and silent yellow
slickers to their knees   blocked the bus and began
                pounding and pounding
on the door with billy clubs   they tore the door off
                and stormed on
dragging the driver off the bus   throwing him in the
                trunk   they said there
wasn't gonna be no demonstration today   not here   but
                once their lights
disappeared   under all that water   someone said let's
                go   so me and Greene
and everyone else got off the anchored bus   and
                walked the four
miles to town   by our soaking selves   When we got to
                McKays   the WHITES
ONLY five&dime   it was empty as a drum   they knew
                we were coming
had locked up and gone home   the street was a
                sea   of umbrellas
and soon as the wind came   which of course it
                did   my threeninetyfive
umbrella blew in on itself   so I left it on the walk a
                broken black
bird   as we started to march towards the city
                council   Greene's fiveninety
five cardboard shoes   began falling apart   we had
                started to cross Main
Street   I could just see the top of the white marble
                building   when about
six cop cars   came wailing out of nowhere   a dozen or
                so plainclothesmen
jumped out   holding these cans of tear gas   they
                said   don't even try
crossing this street   go home and stop making
                trouble   just then the light

changed   turning from red to green   we crossed   the
    men clubbed us
threw their tears at us   they took out our wallets took
    everything we had
and left it on the sidewalk   with our streaming
    eyes   with the rain

Eddie Priest's
Barbershop & Notary
Closed Mondays

is music   is men
off early from work   is waiting
for the chance at the chair
while the eagle claws holes
in your pockets   keeping
time   by the turning
of rusty fans   steel flowers with
cold breezes   is having nothing
better to do   than guess at the years
of hair   matted beneath the soiled caps
of drunks   the pain of running
a fisted comb through stubborn
knots   is the dark dirty low
down blues   the tender heads
of sons fresh from cornrows   all
wonder at losing   half their height
is a mother gathering hair   for good
luck   for a soft wig   is the round
difficulty of ears   the peach
faced boys asking Eddie
to cut in parts and arrows
wanting to have their names read
for just a few days   and among thin
jazz   is the quick brush of a done
head   the black flood around
your feet   grandfathers
stopping their games of ivory
dominoes   just before they reach the bone
yard   is winking widowers announcing
cut it clean off   I'm through courting

and hair only gets in the way   is the final
spin of the chair   a reflection of
a reflection   that sting of wintergreen
tonic   on the neck of a sleeping snow
haired man   when you realize it is
your turn   you are next